BOUNCE

OVERCOMING ADVERSITY, BUILDING RESILIENCE AND FINDING JOY

CASSANDRA GAISFORD

Blue
Giraffe

CONTENTS

PRAISE FOR BOUNCE

"Gently, conversationally, and with humor, *BOUNCE* offers strategies for seeing and thinking differently. For many people the approach is nothing less than transformational."

~ **Lawrence Ford**

"I wouldn't typically use the phrase "something for everybody" in reference to a book, but in this case, the description is apt. Each chapter is like a loving permission slip, and readers will be pulled to the ones they most need to receive. With titles like "Unplug," "Laugh and Play," "Massage," and "Mood Food" the reader receives compelling reasons—followed by implementable steps—for acting on the self-care impulses that most of us dismiss daily.

The author's conversational style makes for easy reading. I am a life coach, and I just added this book to my suggested reading list for my clients."

~ **Sheree Clark, Healthy Living Coach**

"While reading *BOUNCE* I felt that Cassandra had a unique ability to see deep inside me. She met me at where my fears reside, identified with the sources of my stress, and gently challenged me to break free and move through by providing a range of holistic and science-based tools. I especially loved the broad range of tools she covered – from east to west, and esoteric to scientific.

"Cassandra's own explorations are evident in how she connects with the reader. Concepts like I'm broke, I'm lonely, I want to succeed. An easy read chokka full of useful tips for gaining control over your body's reaction to stress. I especially loved the concept of making a list of 'What Not to Do' and developing a 'Miracle Morning Routine'.

"Loved the fact it is an easy read and is so incredibly comprehensive in its spectrum of tools covered: eastern and western/physical and psychological/science and esoteric. It's hard to find books that capture this in one space–a comprehensive manual containing a tasting platter of techniques."

~ **Tina Drummond, Health and Safety Consultant, Wellness Motivator**

"Cassandra has mastered the art of speaking in clear and simple terms and has presented *Bounce* as an easy to read, concise—yet completely comprehensive guide to overcoming all the obstacles that stand between yourself and your passion. She has taken a truly holistic approach and leaves no stone unturned. She lays out all the facets of overcoming your obstacles in a no-nonsense fashion and covers everything ... Mind, body and soul ... the physical, the spiritual, and the scientific. She evens touches on topics that may be considered 'airy-fairy' with believable and inspiring confidence.

While *Bounce* is a concise presentation, do not be fooled by its quick two-hour read, it is incredibly comprehensive astoundingly holistic—and effective. I have been working on a website project for most of this year and over the last couple of months I have been saying that I am almost ready to get on with it, but I keep finding obstacles and excuses to not get real with it. These obstacles and excuses simply amount to allowing myself to listen to the voices of self-doubt that choose to argue in my head. But within days of finishing reading *Bounce* I now have secured my domain name, have my draft website ready to go and I now know that I will be launching it before the end of the year--maybe even within the next few days. As well as being inspiring, motivating and confidence building, Bounce also comes with useful activities and numerous helpful resources to assist you to overcome your obstacles and follow your passion. Cassandra definitely holds your hand but ultimately it is finally up to you to take action. I did, will you?"

~ Niki Firth, 5-Star Review

"*Bounc*e is like a pocket-sized life support that adds a little fun and magic to the experience. Cassandra Gaisford packs a lot of helpful, useful and thoughtful information into this book. Each chapter is sort and the reader can dip in as the mood takes them and find a gem at every stop. One of the many practical strategies I am implementing as a result of reading Bounce is removing all technology from my bedroom. This is a habit born 10 years ago when I was desperate for distraction every minute of my waking day. This is a challenge I am going to rise to.

~ Catherine Sloan, Counselor

"Bounce captures a whole range of meaningful topics, tips & strategies relating to empowering the reader to overcome obstacles build resilience and find their own joy. Simple and transformational ... a personal bible for living ones best life! Cassandra gently supports the reader to 're-programme' their own values and beliefs, creating new habitual ways of thinking from a default mode of operation. A powerful book for every bedside table!"

~ Heather Dodge, Founder Kaleidoscope Solutions

"*Bounce* does not disappoint! It was just the turning point, and encouragement I needed."

"Well-written, thought provoking, and challenges you to step up to the next level of your life in order to succeed!

Do you need to bounce back after a fall? Failed again and wondering what to do next? If so, this book Bounce by Cassandra can help you to make a comeback after experiencing a failure or knockdown.

The book is rich with content that teaches people how to be more resilient in the midst of life's failures and downfalls. In *Bounce* the author teaches you so many strategies and new way of thinking that I can name a handful that are most important to me. For example, we learn the lesson of how to: Dream Big; Follow Your Passion; Find supportive people called 'Bounce Buddies'; Utilize Mind Power; Take Responsibility; Deal With Conflict; Fear Less; Bounce Away From Your Environment; Perform Yoga and Deep Breathing; Prayer Therapy; Laugh and Play

There are a lot more chapters, each short but powerful in its delivery to teaching you how to recover from tough times, become more resilient and charge forward towards greater success.

Bounce is well-written, thought provoking, and challenges you to step up to the next level of your life so that you are never in a position to give up."

DEDICATION

*I dedicate this book to those of you
who are ready to live a more colourful life,
to stress less and do what others may say cannot be done.*

*This book is also for Lorenzo, my Templar Knight,
who encourages and supports me
to make my dreams possible...*

*And for all my clients
who've shared their dreams with me,
and allowed me to help them achieve amazing feats.*

Thank you for inspiring me.

Let's bounce!

PREFACE

"Nothing beautiful in the end comes without a measure of some pain, some frustration, some suffering."

~ His Holiness the Dalai Lama

ABOUT THIS BOOK

This book offers short, sound-bites of stand-alone readings designed to help you cultivate resilience and awareness amid the challenges of daily living.

More than a collection of thoughts for the day, *Bounce: Overcoming Adversity, Building Resilience and Finding Joy* offers a progressive program of holistic—mental, emotional, physical and spiritual—study, guiding you through essential concepts, themes, and practices on the path to well-being, joy, and happiness.

The teachings are gently humorous, sometimes challenging, occasionally provocative, but always compassionate and kind, and, I hope, seemingly infinitely wise.

All that I share are strategies that have worked for me personally through many of my own life challenges, and for my clients in my professional work as a holistic therapist, counsellor, and empowerment coach.

Bounce: Overcoming Adversity, Building Resilience and Finding Joy features the most essential and stirring passages from my previous books, exploring topics such as: meditation, mindfulness, positive health behaviours, and working with fear, depression, anxiety, and other painful emotions. *Bounce* expands upon my previous books in that it encourages a more playful approach to the seriousness of life and the ever-present stressors we all face.

Through the course of this book, you will learn practical, creative and simple methods for heightening awareness and overcoming habitual patterns that block happiness and joy and hold you back.

My hope is that next time you are faced with a setback or adversity, one simple word will come to mind: 'Bounce.' And then, having been reminded that bouncing back from setbacks in a lively manner is the test of your power, that you will then go quickly into resilience mode and apply the strategies you have learned in this book.

If when next faced with a challenge, your default thoughts are 'bounce', and 'how can I bounce?' then I will consider this book a success.

Extra Support: Bounce Companion Workbook

Bounce (the book) offers you information about overcoming adversity, building resilience and finding joy. Reading a book is great but applying the teachings and writing things down in a dedicated space helps bring the learning alive, deepens your self awareness, and enables you to make real world change. Reading gives you knowledge, but reflecting upon and applying that knowledge creates true empowerment.

By writing and recording your responses you're rewriting the story of your life. As Seth Godin states, "Here's the thing: The book that will most change your life is the book you write. The act of writing things down, of justifying your actions, of being cogent and clear, and forthright—that's how you change."

The Bounce Companion Workbook will support you through the learning and show you how to create real and meaningful change in your life...simply and joyfully.

Are you ready to bounce?

Let's get jumping...

INTRODUCTION

Are you feeling flat? Despondent? Stressed or lacking energy? If so, you've come to the right place. It's time to turn up the volume and get your vitality back.

Throughout this book you'll find helpful, timely strategies. As you'll quickly discover, it's all about proactively embracing healthy behaviours. Whether it's your mind, body or soul that needs a lift, you'll see that everything is connected. Even the darkness, despondency and despair.

Without darkness there would be no light. Without winter there would be no summer. Without bad times there would be no happy times. But sometimes, it can be hard to bounce back to reclaim happiness and joy. Life can knock you around. Sometimes it can feel as though setbacks come in unrelenting waves. You can feel like you are drowning in a sea of negativity. You can lose hope. If this feels like you, *Bounce: Overcoming Adversity, Building Resilience and Finding Joy* comes to your rescue.

We are not born with a fixed, unchangeable amount of resilience. It is a muscle that everyone can build, a skill anyone can master. Armed with new knowledge you can rebound from setbacks. You can learn how to find strength in the face of adversity. And you can build your courage muscles and fire up your determination to live a life of passion, love, and joy.

I'm passionate about helping people live prosperous, successful lives, and I care about your health and well-being. People with bounce are happier people and happier people make happier communities.

I hope this book provides some helpful insights and strategies to help you flourish in the wake of any current and future demands you may be experiencing. You'll find strategies that I've used successfully, personally and professionally to find strength in the face of calamity, rebound from setbacks and find joy.

Before we continue, there's just one thing you need to know. This may be a little book, but the concrete steps and practical tools that I'll share in these pages are powerful solutions regardless of your goals, profession, skills, experience, age, and current situation.

They're a seamless blend of ancient wisdom and modern science. They are timeless and limitless, so it's never "too late" or "too soon" to bounce away from despair towards great joy.

So... are you ready? Are you ready to dramatically improve your happiness, success and personal fulfilment? If you've come this far, I think you are...

1

WHAT IS BOUNCE?

Dictionary.com describes 'bounce' as springing back from a surface in a lively manner.

This quality of liveliness, exuberance, and energy is important to keep in mind. The ability to rebound from setbacks, to possess resilience and maintain positive energy, even in the face of calamity, will not just help you survive but, importantly, to thrive in the face of setbacks.

Below are a few other words which encompass the term 'bounce'. You may wish to consider using a few of these in your everyday conversations, to thus adding some pizazz to your day. Or perhaps you may try walking with more exuberance! That could be fun.

- Rebound
- Spring
- Leap
- Resilience
- Vitality
- Energy
- Liveliness
- Recover

- Animation
- Vivacity
- Life
- Spirit
- Pep
- Vigour
- Zip
- Pizazz
- Exuberant
- Bounce off

Whatever is causing you worry or distress, developing a bounce mindset, and increasing your coping skills, will help you reclaim your power and reboot your life.

Bounce your way to happiness. Bounce your way to success. Bounce your way to health. Whatever you do, don't stand still.

2

REAL RESILIENCE

Resilience in action is the ability to spring back to health and readily recover from illness, depression, and adversity. Bouncing back from setbacks is a critical determinant of success in business and life.

Resilience is that indefinable quality that allows some people to be bowled over by life and re-emerge stronger than ever. Rather than letting setbacks overcome them and drain their resolve, they find a way to rise from the ashes.

Psychologists have identified some of the factors that will make you more resilient, among them a positive attitude, optimism, the ability to regulate emotions, and the ability to see failure as a form of helpful feedback.

By strengthening your inner power, your ability to handle stressful situations, and your skill in persevering after setbacks threaten to fell you, you'll develop real resilience—you'll develop grit.

Grit comes in many shapes and sizes: courage, bravery, pluck, mettle, backbone, spirit, steel nerve, resolve, determination, endurance, guts, spunk, tenacity—and the strength of vulnerability. Add the flexibility and determination of resilience and you'll have a powerful bounce strategy.

Life will keep throwing you curveballs—it may even, at times, drown you in a deluge of seemingly never-ending hassles—family dramas, environmental mayhem, world affairs, or some other toxin.

Many of the strategies I'll share with you in this book will help you develop a resilient mindset and with it more staying power, passion, perseverance, and grit.

Mindfulness techniques, avoiding excessive alcohol consumption, keeping your thoughts positive, surrounding yourself with a vibe tribe of positive supporters, getting rid of toxicity (friends, family, or stinkin' thinkin'), meditating, exercise, reprogramming your subconscious beliefs, and other strategies are just some of the things you'll learn in *Bounce: Overcoming Adversity, Building Resilience, and Finding Joy*.

It's not easy to overcome many of the things that hold you back. But you can do it—if you're willing to be strong and fight for your dreams. Within many of us lies an innate seam of strength, which, when mined skilfully, will produce an endless source of pure gold.

As Buddha once said, "It is better to conquer yourself than to win a thousand battles. Then the victory is yours. It cannot be taken from you, not by angels or by demons, heaven or hell."

When you seize the reins of control and take responsibility, you will empower your life, your joy, and your prosperity.

Creating a beautiful mind is one of the most important and effective places you can empower with more bounce.

3

MIND POWER

Your mind is so incredibly vital to the success or failure of virtually everything you do, from relationships, health, work, and finances to overall happiness.

Thoughts do become things, and your body experiences what the mind believes. This is why challenging and conquering your fears and mistaken beliefs is so important.

Happily, you can trick your mind into gravitating towards what you want and away from what you don't.

"I have learned how to deceive people into health for their benefit. Doctors can kill or cure with 'wordswordswords' when they become 'swordswordswords.' We all have the potential for self-induced healing built into us. The key is to know how to achieve your potential," says Bernie Siegel, M.D., author of *A Book of Miracles* and *The Art of Healing*.

Many of the things that influence your thoughts, feelings, and behaviours are invisible; a great many lurk in the realm of the subconscious mind.

The function of your subconscious mind is to store and retrieve data. Its job is to ensure that you respond exactly the way you are programmed.

"By the time you reach the age of 21, you've already permanently stored more than one hundred times the contents of the entire Encyclopaedia Britannica," says motivational writer Brian Tracey.

And much of this information is rubbish, false, incomplete, or obsolete.

Your subconscious mind is like a huge memory bank. Its capacity is virtually unlimited. It permanently stores everything that ever happens to you. What is limited is your ability to consciously recall many of the scripts programmed into your mind.

You may not even be aware of limiting beliefs that are holding you back. Boosting your self-awareness will change that, coupled with a willingness to grow.

One of the most important things you can commit to realising is that you exist in more than the physical world. The mental world, the emotional world, and the spiritual world all exert a powerful influence over you—whether you are consciously tapping into them or not.

"What most people never realise is that the physical realm is merely a 'printout' of the other three," writes T. Harv Eker.

Any limiting and unhelpful beliefs or repressed experiences preventing you from becoming a prosperous author cannot be changed in the physical world. They can only be changed in the "program"—the mental, emotional, and spiritual worlds.

Which is why *Bounce: Overcoming Adversity, Building Resilience, and Finding Joy* takes a holistic approach to health and happiness. Passion, joy, faith, prayer, meditation, courage, dreams, purpose, and mindfulness practices are some of the strategies we'll discuss in this book.

4

CULTIVATE A BOUNCE MINDSET

His Holiness the 14th Dalai Lama once said, "Negative thoughts are like weeds, but positive thoughts are like flowers—they need nurturing every day."

Leonardo da Vinci proactively fertilised his mind and empowered his resolve by focusing on his dreams, goals, and aspirations.

"You cannot help being good, because your hand and your mind, being accustomed to gather flowers would ill know how to pluck thorns," he once wrote.

To steady himself against self-doubt or the attacks of others, he actively cultivated a bounce mindset by using affirmations, journaling, meditating, channeling and accessing the spiritual realms, and surrounding himself with like-minded, aspirational and inspirational people. By doing so, he developed grit and the ability to bounce back from extreme adversity.

If you actively cultivate a success mindset you automatically increase your ability to bounce because your mind will create a barrier to discouragement. This helps bounce back the thorns of self-doubt, procrastination, fear, and any of the other things toxic to your happiness and success.

Oprah once said that one of the best ways to cultivate a success mindset is to think like a queen: "A queen is not afraid to fail. Failure is another stepping stone to greatness."

Similarly, J.K. Rowling encourages making failure part of your success strategy. "Failure is inevitable—make it a strength," she says.

We'll dive deeper into how to fear less and bounce back from failure later in this book.

For now, impress this upon your mind—attitude is everything. As Buddhists say, life is suffering—it's how you react to life that counts. "With our thoughts we make the world," Buddha once said.

Think royal. Cultivate a success mindset and bounce through life like a king or queen.

5

WONDERFUL WINS

Pursue your dreams with the tenacity of a terrier chasing a ball. Create an inspired intention that would fill you with joy when it's achieved.

It doesn't have to be grandiose, it may be as simple as losing excess weight that's dragging you down, taking up an interesting hobby, or asking someone out on a date.

Perhaps, it's having the courage to quit a job you hate and find one you love before it's too late. Or, following your heart's desire and starting a purpose-driven business.

Are you lonely? Would a wonderful win be the willingness to be vulnerable and open your heart to love again?

What matters is that your intention is meaningful and will have a tangible impact on your life. It's something you feel you'd get a lift from saying, "I did that. I did the thing I never thought I could."

Or perhaps, it's proving others' limited expectations of you to be wrong.

If you're unfamiliar with setting inspired intentions here's a simple strategy to help you WIN:

W—What do you want to achieve? Be specific. Make your inspired intention concrete so you can almost see, touch, taste, feel, hear it as being your reality now.

I—Inspiration? What's motivating and inspiring you to win? List as many benefits which will flow when you've achieved your inspired intention.

N—Needs. What are the next steps? What do you need to do or put in place to win? What's your success strategy to ensure you stay on track?

S—Sweet success. What riches or rewards will you reap when you've achieved your inspired intention? Reward yourself with a treat each time you achieve something significant on your journey to success. Dangle a grand prize in front of your nose that will further motivate you to persevere.

I'VE FOUND this simple strategy really helps me create and sustain my bounce. Give it a go and see if it helps you achieve exceptional results too.

Empower your intentions by writing them down, creating a vision board and reviewing your intentions daily. Consider creating a Passion Journal to boost your bounce and manifest your intentions. You'll find some helpful tips in the last chapter of this book.

Don't be afraid to bounce too high. Amplify your feelings of satisfaction and success by dreaming big, achieving something audacious and lifting your sights even higher.

6

DREAM BIG

"Dream big," encourages James Patterson, currently the bestselling author in the world. "Don't set out to write a good thriller. Set out to write a #1 thriller."

Patterson, whose father was raised in a poorhouse, knows the power of big dreams and passionate perseverance. His first book was turned down by 21 publishers and won The Edgar for Best First Mystery. He also quit a lucrative legal career because it didn't make him bounce.

Given that science has barely even begun to explore the real potential of the human mind, it's a funny thing how easily we persuade ourselves of its limitations and settle for less.

You've probably caught yourself thinking about a big dream, some inspired course of action, and at some point talked yourself down by saying, "I could never do that!"

Or perhaps you've come up with a bright idea about something and then shelved it because somebody said dismissively, "You can't do that!" or "That's crap."

Or perhaps, as I have so often said to myself before reconnecting with my millionaire mindset, "I can't do this. I can't write this book.

It's too big. Who do I think I am trying to write such a complex book?"

But how do you really know what you are capable of unless you try?

Paulo Coehlo, the author of *The Alchemist*, once said: "Know what you want and try to go beyond your own expectations. Improve your dancing, practice a lot, and set a very high goal, one that will be difficult to achieve. Because that is an artist's million: to go beyond one's limits. An artist who desires very little and achieves it has failed in life."

Thinking big demands a long step outside the comfort zone of what you know.

It can feel scary to contemplate stepping out of the space where you feel you know what you're doing and you feel fully in control.

It can feel frightening to explore what it would be like if you were to leave the comfort rut and attempt to climb toward a new summit. You don't know for sure where it will lead. But everyone who's ever made a success of anything started with a big dream.

And you can, too.

Tim Ferris dreams big by adopting and cherishing his beginner's mind. Rather than succumb to the fear of failure, he changes his mindset, and affirms his love of variety and challenge and being a perpetual debutante.

"Think small, to go big" encourages Gary Keller in his book *The One Thing*. "Going small" is ignoring all the things you could do and doing what you should do.

"It's recognising that not all things matter equally and finding the things that matter most. It's a tighter way to connect what you do with what you want. It's realising that extraordinary results are directly determined by how narrow you can make a focus."

When you think too big, achieving success can feel overwhelming, time-consuming, and complicated. Calendars can become overloaded and success starts to feel out of reach. So, people opt out and either quit or settle for less.

"Unaware that big success comes when we do a few things well, they get lost trying to do too much, and in the end, accomplish too little," says Keller.

"Over time they lower their expectations, abandon their dreams, and allow their life to get small. This is the wrong thing to make small."

Every extraordinary achievement starts as someone's daydream. Dream big, become audaciously obsessed, and fuel your verve— pursue the vision that sparkles and get ready to bounce!

7
BOUNCE HIGH

Don't be afraid of attracting attention by bouncing too high. Think of the gold standard you'll set for others who will be inspired by your success.

If you bounce too high others will notice you. They may become jealous and try and sabotage your success. Don't feel you have to bounce low and go with the status quo.

If people try to pop your balloon, remind yourself of why you are bouncing and what you are trying to achieve. This will help strengthen your courage and commitment to achieving your fullest potential.

If you decide you are going to become a bouncer there will be people who will try and slow you down. It's not nice, but it does happen. Think ahead and develop strategies along the way so others don't dampen your efforts.

Perhaps you could think like the bouncers in a pub. These body-guards are there to stop the unwanted from spoiling things. You need to have your own bouncers in your toolkit. That way when the unwanted arrive you'll already know how to deal with them. You may try and defuse things or get potential saboteurs on board, or you may need to be firmer and bounce them off somewhere else.

SELF-SOOTHE

When you feel flat or worried your default thoughts can veer toward the negative. You may find yourself saying, *"I'm broke. I won't succeed. Everyone is out to get me. I'm lonely. I'm useless."* Or something else discouraging.

The trouble is, these negative affirmations will become your reality. And you don't want that to happen, do you?

To affirm something is declaring it to be true. an affirmation is also a statement you intend to be true. Listen to your words—are your intentions setting you up for failure or success?

Claim back your power and self-soothe. Harness the power of positive affirmations to convince yourself you'll succeed or get through whatever is troubling you. Create and hold a vision for what you know, or wish can be true.

"I am the greatest," Muhammad Ali used to say repeatedly. "I said that even before I knew I was. I figured that if I said it enough, I would convince the world that I really was the greatest."

A superhero in and out of the boxing ring Mohammed Ali was a fast-talking world-conquering superhero (1942 - 2016).

Similarly, many people experiencing profound grief or trauma often turn to affirmations for comfort. "All is well. Everything is working out for my highest good," Louise Hay, the author of *You Can Heal Your Life*, used to say. "Out of this situation, only good will come."

As you'll discover later the power of hope is a magical thing.

Affirmations repeated regularly work because they program your mind and activate the part of the brain that acts as a filter—registering what's important to you and screening out what you no longer value.

Another reason affirmations work is that they create a dynamic tension. If what you are affirming has more bounce than what you currently believe, the tension between the two different realities becomes uncomfortable.

To rid yourself of the tension you can either accept the status quo and stop saying the affirmation or raise your reality and bounce higher by making the affirmation and reality match.

Plant your affirmations deeper by framing them emotionally. Instead of, "Obstacles do not bend me", experiment with "I feel strong in the face of obstacles they do not bend me", for example.

Or, "I am joyfully building greater resilience, every day I grow stronger."

These emotion-laden statements engage your heart-centre so that deeper, more resilient changes can take root.

Deeper changes create greater, habitual, instinctive bounce.

FOLLOW YOUR PASSION

Passion is a source of unlimited energy from your soul that enables you to achieve extraordinary results. It's the fire that ignites your potential and inspires you to be who you really are.

Following your passion and claiming your authentic self is a great way to boost your vitality. Whether you call it joy, love or obsession or desire, these powerful heart-felt emotions are natural opiates for your mind, body, and soul.

Sadly, when you're feeling anxious, depressed or stressed, the things that you love are the first things to be traded. Nothing seems to spark joy. But, when you do something that feeds your soul you may be amazed at how quickly fire ignites.

Passion brings the energy or chi of love, giving you energy, vitality and a heightened sense of well-being. It's one of the greatest stress-busters of all and promotes the generation of endorphins—feel-good chemicals that will give you an extra spring in your step.

Your passion may start as a hobby or as a way to cure your blues, but could very well turn out to be your ticket to a more fulfilling career.

That's how things rolled for Claire Robbie. Robbie was a news reporter on TV3's *Nightline* before a tumultuous time led her to discover the life-changing benefits of yoga and meditation.

At a low point in her life, what started as a way of healing became an essential part of her recovery process, and as her love for her new practices grew, so did the sense that she had discovered a new vocation.

She now has a career-combo as a meditation and yoga teacher and part-time journalist. Robbie says she loves helping people take, "the amazing step towards living more mindfully."

What do you love doing? What inspires you? What makes you feel joyful? Identify these things and make some time to follow your passion. Even five minutes a day doing something you love can give you back your mojo.

10

FIND AND FOLLOW YOUR PURPOSE

If you want to create more bounce in your life finding and following your purpose is another good place to invest time and energy.

However, this is an area where many people struggle. The US Center for Disease Control recently reported that 40% of Americans have not discovered a satisfying life purpose, and lack any idea of what makes their lives purposeful and meaningful.

It is well known that having purpose and meaning in your life increases not only life satisfaction but also promotes mental and physical health.

Many successful authors, for example, testify to the power of writing with purpose and sharing their stories and purpose-driven words.

So, where and how do you find your life purpose? "The wound is where the light comes in", said the Persian poet and mystic Rumi. Many people have found their life purpose following their recovery from trauma or adversity of some kind.

"It is in giving that I connect with others, with the world and with the divine", says author Isabel Allende. Following the death of her daughter, who fell into a coma in 1991 and never recovered, she poured her grief onto the page and wrote a memoir as a tribute to

Paula's life. She still receives letters from people who tell her how much her book, *Paula,* helped them through their own grief.

Self-help icon Louise Hay's personal philosophy was forged from her tormented upbringing. Her childhood was unstable and impoverished, and her teen years were marked by abuse. Louise started what would become her life's work in New York City in 1970.

Hay attended meetings at the Church of Religious Science and began training in the ministerial program. She became a popular speaker at the church and soon found herself counselling clients. This work quickly blossomed into a full-time career.

After several years, Louise compiled a reference guide detailing the mental causes of physical ailments and developed positive thought patterns for reversing illness and creating health. This compilation was the basis for Heal Your Body is also known affectionately as "The Little Blue Book."

I forged a successful career helping people find their passion and purpose following negative work experiences that robbed my self-esteem and threatened my health and vitality. My purpose? To encourage and inspire others. And help people live and work with beauty and joy.

Your life purpose may not evolve from the transcendence of your own wounds, but it's incredibly fulfilling when your life purpose empowers others. That's bounce!

If you need more help to find and live your life purpose you can read my book, *Find Your Passion and Purpose: Four Easy Steps to Discover a Job You Want and Live the Life You Love*, available as a paperback and Ebook.

Or you may prefer to take my online course and watch inspirational and practical videos and other strategies to help you to fulfil your potential—https://the-coaching-lab.teachable.com/p/follow-your-passion-and-purpose-to-prosperity.

11

JUMPING WITH JOY

Joy has phenomenal energy and incredible versatility. In *The Book of Joy* the Dalai Lama shares that Paul Ekman, a longtime friend and famed emotions researcher, has written that joy is associated with feelings as varied as:

- Pleasure (of the five senses)
- Amusement (from a chuckle to a belly laugh)
- Contentment (a calmer kind of satisfaction)
- Excitement (in response to novelty or challenge)
- Relief (following upon another emotion, such as fear, anxiety, and even pleasure)
- Wonder (before something astonishing and admirable)
- Ecstasy or bliss (transporting us outside ourselves)
- Exultation (at having accomplished a difficult or daring task)
- Radiant pride (when our children earn a special honour)
- Elevation (from having witnessed an act of kindness, generosity, or compassion)
- Gratitude (the appreciation of a selfless act of which one is the beneficiary)

Buddhist scholar and former scientist Matthieu Ricard has added three other more exalted states of joy: rejoicing (in someone else's happiness, what Buddhists call *mudita*) delight or enchantment (a shining kind of contentment) spiritual radiance (a serene joy born from deep well-being and benevolence).

When you tap into your joy, you tap into an unlimited reservoir of energy and enthusiasm.

The French take it further—of course! *Jouissance*, literally means orgasmic joy. It's derived from the word from *jouir* ("to enjoy"). *Jouissance* is to enjoy something a lot!

One of my favourite creativity experts Mihaly Czikszentmihaly, refers to this as a state of "flow."

In a popular YouTube talk he asks, "What makes a life worth living? Money cannot make us happy," he says. Instead, he urges us to learn from people who find pleasure and lasting satisfaction in activities that bring about this state of transcendent flow.

Coco Chanel was flowing when she designed her clothes, she was flowing when she attended to the minutest details of her garments. For her, her work had a spiritual aspect, it wasn't a job, it was her vocation and her deepest purpose—to liberate women from corsets and clothes that constricted their freedom.

"Ask someone born under the sign of Leo about the secret of leadership or a successful life and they will invariably list passion and tenacity, and a predisposition towards joy as the proper tools for the job," writes Steven Weiss in his book, *Signs of Success: The Remarkable Power of Business Astrology.*

As a Leo, Coco Chanel exemplified this. She knew that you can succeed at almost anything if you follow your joy. This is where your soul meets the road—accelerating you toward your preferred future and fuelling your success.

Find something that sparks joy and keep hugely interested in it by feeding and nurturing your *jouissance* every day.

Encourage yourself, challenge any mistaken assumptions and boost your belief by collecting examples of people who followed their joy and made a rewarding career or enriched their lives.

12

EFFORTLESS BLISS

Some of the most common questions I'm asked by people who seeking coaching is, "How can I find out what I'm good at? What are my talents?" and "How can I be sure that I will enjoy it and succeed?"

Whilst the answers may be evasive, the past is often a good predictor of the future. Often you just need reminding of the times and circumstances in your life when you felt inspired or energised by something, when your skills just seemed to flow, and of the outcomes, successes and positive feedback you achieved. These moments of bounce provide important clues to your passions and unique strengths and talents.

Effortless bliss happens without force. It's the sheer state of joy and transcendence you experience when you're in that state of flow which I referred to in the previous chapter.

When you follow your bliss, some people believe this is where our capacity for genius resides. "The Greeks believed our genius was not part of us but was a divine visitation.

"Our jobs, as artists and writers, was to become the best possible vessel for that genius. Part of that is to be forever learning, improving, expanding, and experimenting," writes Jessa Crispin in her fabulous book, *The Creative Tarot: A Modern Guide to an Inspired Life.*

Bliss is the home of our God-given talents, and to activate their potential and reap the benefits we need to bring them out to play.

"The accompanying state of joy is quite distinct from the thrill of success; it is a joy of inner peace and oneness with all of life," writes David Hawkins in his fabulous book, *Power vs. Force: The Hidden Determinants of Human Behaviour.*

To reach this state of bliss often requires a willingness to step outside your current comfort zone and challenge yourself to soar beyond what you know.

"It is notable that this transcendence of the personal self and surrender to the very essence or spirit of life often occur at a point just beyond the apparent limit of the athlete's ability," says Hawkins.

I experienced this when I embarked on my first attempt at writing a historical novel. Some of the early feedback I received included, "Sheer brilliance." No one was more surprised than me.

The words and ideas just seemed to flow.

"This phenomenon," says Hawkins, "Is commonly described in terms of pushing oneself to the point where one suddenly breaks through a performance barrier and the activity then miraculously becomes effortless; the body then seems to move with grace and ease of its own accord, as though animated by some invisible force."

I also lose all track of time when I am painting. The most fulfilling part of this is creating something that is innately satisfying to me and that the recipient truly loves. I feel excited, energised, and truly complete.

I feel a huge sense of purpose and people comment positively about my flow-inspired works and tell me how something I created changed their life.

Writing books, posts and articles that help people to follow their bliss comes easily to me and produces the same state.

I won an art award once, and my first attempt at an oil painting was selected as a finalist in a prestigious portraiture award. It seemed so effortless that I was completely thrown.

I don't say this to boast, but I wanted to share with you that in both cases, and many more, I always experienced self-doubt, and I never possessed the confidence or believed I had talent, but I did what made my soul sing, and challenged myself to show up and share my work anyway.

Perhaps you may set yourself a similar 'stretch' goal, or you may be blissfully content to explore what energises you and keep your talents hidden. Either way, it is in the act of following your bliss that you will find great joy and personal fulfilment.

13

BEAUTIFUL BOUNCE

Your Beautiful Mind

When you feel love, joy, gratitude, awe, curiosity, bliss, playfulness, ease, creativity, compassion, growth, or appreciation, you're in your beautiful mind.

Your beautiful mind is in a stream of transcendence and flow. Your spirit and your heart are aligned, and your best self comes alive. Nothing feels like a hassle, everything feels peaceful. You feel no fear or frustration. You're in harmony with your true essence.

Your Suffering Mind

When you're feeling stressed out, worried, frustrated, angry, anxious, depressed, irritable, overwhelmed, resentful, or fearful, your suffering mind has taken control.

Negative feelings and emotions become the norm, even if you'd prefer they weren't.

As I wrote at the beginning of this book, his Holiness the Dalai Lama reminds us, "Nothing beautiful in the end comes without a measure of some pain, some frustration, some suffering."

As I write this chapter, my partner and I are in the midst of our house renovations. A beautiful tree was too ill to be saved. It was devastating to see it felled. It would have been easy to focus on the ugliness of the clay, and mud, and debris its removal has left behind. Instead, I turn my attention to the new vision of what will grow—of the beauty which will come again.

Reframe your uglies. Take back control, find and prioritise the beauties—the things that spark joy, that give you pleasure and bring deep satisfaction to your mind, body, and soul.

These may be sensory delights, like the smell of fresh coffee, or freshly cut grass, or a whiff of your favourite perfume. Perhaps a stunning photo or a painting sparks joy, or a fabulous piece of architecture. Or, the vivid blue of a summer sky.

Look for the beauty within things you may associate with ugliness. Acknowledge any pain, frustration and suffering as a rite of passage and find beauty in life to reclaim your bounce.

14

SLOW BOUNCE

While we're on the subject of effortlessness, it seems important to talk about peaceful patience. So many people equate speed with progress. Yet, there's something refined and graceful and enduring about things that take their time to flower.

Savour your journey, enjoy the ride, be kind to yourself and be patient during setbacks. Rejoice in steady progress, no matter how small. Slowly chip away at the things most important to you. Learn and grow from any challenges, but don't let them stop you.

Crawl, creep, dally, dawdle or go a the pace of a snail—whatever your tempo, incremental movements forward still equal progress.

Revel in the slow bounce by looking back and appreciating what you have already achieved and how many lives you have positively impacted along the way. Keep your focus away from any lapses you may think you've made. Berating yourself or piling on the guilt won't speed your progress.

Forgive yourself for what you think you've done or haven't done or how little progress you feel you've made. Take heart from Leonardo da Vinci and other enduring icons of success. It's not how quickly you get there, it's the enduring legacy you leave behind that matters most.

15

BOUNCE BUDDIES

The simplest definition of bounce buddies is a group of supportive people that share the same values, beliefs, and aspirations.

Your bounce buddies are the ones who always have your back no matter how flat or down you feel. They're the ones that you show your vulnerable, wounded, self-doubting self and they still love and support you unconditionally—worry warts and all.

Your bounce buddies can also help motivate, and reenergise you and cheerlead your successes.

As you've already discovered, sometimes to flourish you need to break free of your current tribe and find one that breathes fresh air into your life, lifts you higher and brings out the best in you. Your best-fit bounce buddies are committed co-creators in one another's mutual success.

Your bounce buddies are a great team of supportive others— whether they be significant friends, partners, or family members, or those found online through wonderful Facebook groups and webinars. They may even be your clients.

I found many of my bounce buddies online when I devoted myself to living and working with passion. We've never met in person, but we stay connected and share success strategies via Facebook, emails and occasionally we link-up on video conferencing calls.

One of my key cheerleaders is my partner, Lorenzo. We got together over lunch one day and bounced some ideas around for this book.

When you choose to step out of limiting thoughts and open your heart to others, you'll find the people who want to share and celebrate the journey with you. You'll find your bounce buddies.

Before I sat down to write this chapter, I reached out to my bounce buddies and asked if anyone would like to be an advance reader.

I received so much interest and encouragement. Email responses like the one I received from Robert reminded me of my higher purpose. "Sounds just what I need at the moment."

"I'd be happy to help out. Love your work and recommend it to others at least once a week!" replied Chrissie.

And Catherine, who offered her enthusiastic support, "I will give up sleep to do this for you —I love what I have read so far - YES - pick me."

This feedback, plus the positive reviews on both Amazon and the Facebook communities I have created for my readers , sustains me and encourages me to keep writing. I love hearing their success stories too.

Other readers have become bounce buddies by reaching out to me and interviewing me on their podcasts and success summits. Recently, Sheree Clark, a fabulous and influential healthy-living coach based in the US, discovered my book *Mid-life Career Rescue: The Call for Change* and showcased it on American television.

She also included an interview with me in her fabulous "What the Fork" summit. You'll find a link to this interview and the TV clip on my media page at www.cassandragaisford.com/media.

Successful authors and podcasters like Tim Ferris (tim.blog/podcast) and Joanna Penn (www.thecreativepenn.com) found their bounce buddies by following their enthusiasms and passionate purposes to share what they learn with others.

Here are a few ways to find your bounce buddies:

• Scan Facebook for like-minded groups

• Enrol in an online course that sparks your interest or is teaching a skill you'd love to master—they often include a private members group on social media

• Create a Facebook community of your own—show up and encourage others

• Listen to podcasts which inspire you to become the best version of you. Tim Ferriss' podcast is always inspiring http://tim.blog/podcast. I also love Emily Thompson and Kathleen Shannon's Being Boss podcast; Hilary Henderschoott's Profit Boss; and Devi Adea's Spiritual Entrepreneur

• Check out Meetup.com and find a group of like-minded souls to meet up with in person

• Speak from your heart, and reach out to those you love, or feel could help

If you're having trouble bouncing, there are many networks within the community that can assist you. This could be your local Church, the LifeLine Service, or the services offered to the community by your Local Council, e.g., Citizens Advice Bureau.

Your own friends and family could also be a great help if you are willing to listen to their suggestions.

Remember, "A problem shared is a problem halved." Gather a team of supportive or like-minded people who will nourish your burning desire, cheerlead, and support you when you feel flat or overwhelmed and who get a buzz from helping you succeed.

16

SORT IT

Sometimes life can feel like an obstacle race. Having things in your way will slow down your ability to bounce and can completely stop you in your tracks.

Things in your way could be things you have to do but put off doing. For example, revamping your resume, having conversations that are a little uncomfortable, or paying bills.

If you don't sort them, not only will they prevent you from being able to bounce, but ongoing procrastination, denial and putting your head in the sand will leave you feeling despondent and flat.

Get things sorted without delay. Tackle the things you least want to do first—they are usually your biggest rocks. But the payoff and rewards for completing these tasks can be liberating.

Rather than have a to-do list you may decide to put in place a not to do list.

'What should we simplify?'" Tim Ferris writes in his bestselling book, *Tools of Titans*. "Adding elements to your business strategy is often expensive and time-consuming but removing things isn't."

Ferriss says, "I've since applied this 'What if I could only subtract ...?' to my life in many areas, and I sometimes rephrase it as 'What should I put on my not-to-do list?'"

Here are some of the things many successful people vow **not** to do, or do less of, to stress less and be more empowered:

• Procrastinating
• Working on tasks that are low value
• Doing small things first
• Surfing the internet incessantly
• Not paying bills on time
• Spending too long on Facebook and social media
• Getting involved in extra activities
• Relentless perfectionism
• Avoiding facing issues or seeking help

Decluttering is another simple, but effective way, to simplify your life. Your environment very often mirrors your inner world. Chaos leads to stress and exhaustion, ending in physical and emotional depletion.

When faced with overwhelm sometimes the best place to start is somewhere simple.

Perhaps the sock drawer. Just how many mismatched socks is it possible to store? The windows, just how much brighter is your room once the grime has been removed? These, and other simple steps will yield immediate results.

"There is a calm that can ascend when we're quietly busy with seemingly mundane tasks. Our minds are free to drift and muse, and in the spaciousness of busyness, new solutions to old problems have room to appear," says Melanie Spears, creator of *The Gratitude Diary*.

Declutter. Embrace the elemental art of simplicity. Remove things from your life that don't spark joy. Do the important things and ignore the trivial—it will make a real difference to your energy levels, your life and your career.

17

TAKE RESPONSIBILITY

Whatever is going on in your life you must take personal responsibility. You may not be able to change the circumstances, But changing yourself is something you can control.

It can take courage to take ownership of your health, happiness, and success. Taking responsibility can mean ending years of blaming others.

Taking responsibility is the ultimate of freedoms. The freedom to be yourself and to choose what happens to you. Coco Chanel once said that she didn't want to weigh more heavily on a man than a bird. She fought for her independence and created an enduring fortune in the process.

But it's not just about the money. People who take complete responsibility for their lives often experience profound joy and the confidence and the added security of knowing they are in the driving seat.

They are able to make wise choices because they know they have ultimate responsibility for those choices and can control how they react to setbacks.

If blaming others or making excuses plays repeatedly in your mind, you are shifting **responsibility** for your decisions and life to others. It's time for some tough and compassionate self-love.

- Eliminate blame, eliminate excuses.
- Commit to an excuse-free diet. Take one hundred percent responsibility for your actions, your thoughts, and your goals. Monitor and be a guard for your words, thoughts and actions.
- Spend time thinking about, and taking action towards your goals, dreams, and desires. Become audaciously inspired and empowered by your visions of success.
- Live every day as if what you do matters—because it does. Every choice you make; every action you take—matters. Your choices matter to you and to the life you live.
- Bounce higher—create your best life by taking back control.

18

ELIMINATE NEGATIVE EMOTIONS

Toxic emotions, including anxiety, depression, anger, and resentment, if left unresolved, are insidious thieves of energy and vitality.

Avoid Groundhog Day. Don't let people, things, or situations which trigger unhealed wounds or that spark irritability take you prisoner. Pinpoint the causes and look for solutions.

Resist the urge to play "victim." In the short term, it may seem like the easy option, but long term, this unresolved source of stress will create havoc on your mind, body, and soul.

Anger prepares your body to fight, and it does a lot of damage to your brain and body if you're in a situation where you sustain those stress chemicals. The Thymus gland begins to shrivel up and this can make you susceptible to internal organ ulceration.

Anger can even kill you. A new study in the journal *Social Science and Medicine* found that the angrier you are the most likely you are to have health problems and die early.

Furthermore, when you trigger the stress response by getting angry, it effectively disengages the thinking part of the brain, the cerebral cortex – which is fine if you need to launch into combat. Though it doesn't help if you need to choose the best response, to stop and muse on the merits of your chosen course of action.

There is incredibly wide-spread ignorance of how emotions actually work. People struggle with the idea that we can choose our emotions. It is impossible for anyone to make another person angry, sad, depressed, or happy—without their consent. There is always a point of choice, no matter how fleeting this decisive moment may seem.

Drowning in a sea of negativity or keeping baggage from the past will leave no room for happiness in the future.

Avoid choices which weaken your life energy: shame, guilt, confusion, fear, hatred, pride, hopelessness, and falsehood. Embrace those that lift you higher: truth, courage, acceptance, reason, love, beauty, joy, and peace.

If you're struggling to deal with negative emotions there's a wealth of help on hand. Self-help your way to success; talk to a supportive, wise friend, or seek advice from a counsellor, psychologist, life coach, or another expert. Remember, "a problem shared is a problem solved."

Consider reading my *Millionaire Mindset* book. Even though it was written for authors, the strategies apply to anyone who wants to overcome negative emotions and develop more empowering beliefs.

19

CHANGE THE WAY YOU REACT

By change of reaction comes a change of circumstance, say many great spiritual masters and teachers. If you are distressed or feeling anxious or in a low mood, taking back control can prove challenging. It is hard to feel energised and optimistic when you are overwhelmed, depleted, and despairing.

It's hard—but not impossible. Viktor Frankl, an Austrian psychiatrist who survived the horrors of Nazi death camps, believed that it's not the situation which defines and controls us, but our attitudes and reactions. The key to his survival, Frankl maintained, was searching for meaning in that which seems unfathomable.

Stressed or not, you can determine your reaction. "Between stimulus and response, there is a space. In that space is our power to choose our response. In our response lies our growth and our freedom," Frankl said. Ensure success at becoming less stressed and more empowered by:

• Focusing on three good things you have done each day
• Praising yourself when you achieve a result
• Practicing radical acceptance of yourself, or the situation, if you feel stressed

• Find meaning and purpose in your experience.

In my book *Stress Less. Love Life More: How to Stop Worrying, Reduce Anxiety, Eliminate Negative Thinking and Find Happiness*, I shared strategies to help you transcend the biological stress reaction before it overpowers you. Listed below are two simple strategies:

Reinterpret the situation: e.g., change the meaning; instead of "they should do what I want," try, "I'm learning how to cope with other peoples' demands."

Modify or remove the stressor/s: e.g., assertive action; prioritise; work reasonable hours; quit a job you hate.

Bounce back from setbacks and proactivity choose high-vibration responses. As David Hawkins writes in *Power vs. Force*, "Love is more powerful than hatred; truth sets you free; forgiveness liberates both sides; unconditional love heals; courage empowers, and the essence of Divinity/Reality is peace."

20

BOUNCE MEMORIES THAT SUCK

If you change your beliefs you will change your life. That's great to know—but how do you do that in a way that lasts?

To better understand why some memories create disempowering beliefs that are hard to shift, let's take a wee wander around the brain.

Stressful or emotionally intense experiences stimulate hormones that activate parts of the brain associated with housing memories and emotions. The secretion of epinephrine (adrenaline) and cortisol stimulate the amygdala.

The amygdala, in turn, stimulates the hippocampus and the cerebral cortex, which are both important for memory storage. However, excessive or prolonged stress, with correspondingly prolonged cortisol, impairs memory.

This explains why people find it so difficult to forget traumatic and stressful events—often replaying them again and again in their minds. The emotional charge that the event held consolidates and strengthens the memory into long-term storage.

If the traumatic event is not processed and worked through, the emotional charge remains, locking it further in the cellular structure of the brain. Counselling or reprogramming using hypnosis are some of the many techniques that may be necessary to help you **change your view of the event.**

For example, one effective and powerful counselling technique used to assist people who are suffering from Post-Traumatic Stress Disorder is called "Rapid Eye Desensitization." It works by removing/altering the previous biochemical or structural change the trauma of the event created.

While counselling and reframing techniques, in general, can help you to gain a new perspective, "Rapid Eye Desensitization" weakens the emotional charge.

Shifting Self-Limiting Beliefs

Traumatic memories leave a residue of unhelpful beliefs; yet so often, we aren't even aware of what our self-limiting beliefs are. If your unhelpful thoughts are ingrained, or you keep sabotaging your own success, seeking help from a qualified practitioner with expertise in reprogramming stubborn, disempowering beliefs may be a game-changer.

A wonderful counsellor who I trained to be a Worklife Solutions Certified Life Coach recommended the book *The Biology of Belief: Unleashing the Power of Consciousness, Matter & Miracles*, by Bruce Lipton.

Lipton is an American developmental biologist best known for promoting the idea that genes and DNA can be manipulated by a person's beliefs.

In his book, he shares how he experienced a paradigm shift while at a conference. Back then, Lipton, like so many of us, didn't fully realise the crucial role the subconscious mind plays in the change process.

"Instead, I relied mostly on trying to power through negative behaviour, using positive thinking and willpower. I knew, though, that I had had only limited success in making personal changes in my own life.

"I also knew that when I offered this solution, the energy in the room dropped like a lead balloon. It seems my sophisticated audiences had already tried willpower and positive thinking with limited success."

Fate intervened for Lipton, as it did for me when I was guided to his book. So often life whispers to us, but we fail to tune in. In Lipton's case, the messenger he needed to hear was sitting right next to him; psychotherapist Rob Williams, the creator of the self-help tool PSYCH-K, was presenting at the same conference.

"Rob's opening remarks quickly had the entire audience on the edge of our seats. In his introduction, Rob stated that PSYCH-K can change long-standing, limiting beliefs in a matter of minutes," Lipton wrote.

In his book *The Biology of Belief*, Lipton shares how, in less than 10 minutes, a woman paralysed by her fear of public speaking transformed into a confident, excited, and visibly relaxed person up on the stage. The transformation Lipton witnessed was so astounding, he has since used PYSCH-K in his own life.

"PSYCH-K has helped me undo my self-limiting beliefs, including one about not being able to finish my book," Lipton wrote at the end of his book.

That struck a chord with me. I felt a trill of excitement. Not a thrill, but a trill—a song deep in my heart. Lipton was like the Pied Piper and I was happy to follow. At the time, I had so many unfinished books and had published nothing.

A month after working with a PSYCH-K trained practitioner, I finished the first two books in my *Mid-Life Career Rescue* series. Soon after, I released my third, *Midlife Career Rescue: Employ Yourself*, followed quickly by a fourth book, *How to Find Your Passion and Purpose*.

At the time of writing, I have also published three romance books under my pen name, Mollie Mathews.

Now, (at the time of writing) you're reading my sixteenth book—all completed within the last two years. All because, despite feeling skeptical (and a little vulnerable), I sought help to reprogram my mindset.

If traumatic memories or unhelpful beliefs are ingrained, or you keep sabotaging your own success, seeking help from a qualified practitioner with expertise in reprogramming stubborn, disempowering beliefs may be a game-changer.

You may not need to see a therapist to move beyond self-limiting beliefs; but if you do, go and get help. There's magic in that.

You can also learn from some of the most powerful, effective, and simple techniques used by practitioners working in the realm of positive psychology and mind reprogramming. This includes hypnosis—something you'll discover in the next chapter.

21

HAPPY HYPNOSIS

UK based hypnotherapist Marissa Peer says that there are only three things you need to know about your mind: it likes what is familiar, it responds to the pictures in your head, and it gravitates to what you desire.

To get the tremendous power of your unconscious mind behind your goals, you will need to program it for success. A simple and exceedingly effective way to do this is through hypnosis.

"Emotional problems work much more on the 'feeling level' than the 'thinking level' which is why just trying to think differently is so hard," say the UK-based hypnotherapists at Uncommon Knowledge.

"We use hypnosis to help you feel different quickly which then makes you think differently about a situation."

You can access hypnosis sessions from the comfort of your home via instant download. There's an endless array of scripts on offer to help you overcome self-doubt, increase confidence, reduce anxiety, overcome addictions and much more.

But a word of caution first—the Internet is awash with websites which offer hypnosis products and services that have not been created by experienced and qualified professionals. Some of these programs are of limited or no use, while others may do more harm than good.

"Hypnosis is the epitome of mind-body medicine. It can enable the mind to tell the body how to react and modify the messages that the body sends to the mind," reported the *New York Times* in a recent article.

Harness the power of your mind to put weight into your dreams, and to help you remove obstacles to your success. Experiment with this powerful technique and reprogram your subconscious mind for success.

Don't forget about the transformational power of self-hypnosis, affirmations and the self-soothing strategies I shared previously. Kind, encouraging, and sometimes stroppy self-talk can really help you bounce. Talk yourself up and enjoy a natural high.

22

GOOD VIBRATIONS

My daughter Hannah Joy is contributing this chapter about the power of music to help you bounce. Hannah is a gifted writer with an AMAZING voice, and an instinctive feel for music. Before she could walk or talk she would jive along to her favourite songs—one of which was Mustang Sally from the movie *The Commitments*. Here's what she wrote:

There are so many ways that music can help you and heal you. It's the reason people train to become music therapists. But you don't need to have a degree to benefit from good vibrations.

As a young girl, I would spend countless hours dancing around my room to my iPod pretending I was at the Video Music Awards or the Grammys. Music helped me to escape my reality, but at the same time, I was able to work with the Law of Attraction and manifest better things.

I spent countless hours pretending I was on a film set, singing songs. When I was 25-years-old I manifested the opportunity of a lifetime—to appear in a feature-length musical film. It was recorded in Peter Jackson's studio in Miramar, Wellington, and involved the New Zealand Symphony Orchestra. I was so excited!

Pythagoras was the first known person to use Music Therapy to help people with mental afflictions. This practice has been used to overcome adversity for thousands of years.

We first begin to respond to music in the womb. In the last trimester as babies, we are able to hear musical sounds.

We develop our innate capacity to move to a beat and to feel a beat. The rhythm of our mother's heartbeat is the first beat we respond to as foetuses.

(I recall that before she was born Hannah used to rock to 'Mustang Sally' by The Commitments).

Tones and sounds affect our psychology. Listening to peaceful music can help you to sleep just as upbeat music can lift your mood. If I ever feel sad I put on a happy song.

Music can be used for comfort. Music can be used to empower the passage of sadness. Music can induce a relaxation response— especially some classical music.

It's not just the melodies though, it's also the lyrics and the stories people tell with their words. For me, the lyrics in Taylor Swift's 1989 album helped me to overcome a terrible breakup.

Her vulnerability and the rawness of her lyrics were so uplifting for me. It helped me feel less alone in my experience to know that she had felt the same confusions and frustrations too. This was the album where she released the song "Shake it Off."

Shaking it off is a brilliant way to bounce back. Sometimes we get far too bogged down in reality and we simply need to return to our inner child and have some fun. Plug in those headphones, put a happy playlist on Spotify and dance around the house.

Crystal bowls are one of the most powerful musical healers. These bowls send sound vibrations through the room that have healing energies that vibrate through our bodies.

It's actual physics, so there is science behind this. Just like Shaman healers use drums for their healing purposes. Sound healing has been used around the globe for centuries.

The didgeridoo is considered one of the world's oldest musical instruments. This instrument is fast becoming accepted as a form of treatment for sleep apnea. This instrument of the indigenous Australians facilitates meditation, states of harmony and balance—among other bouncy things!

Sound healing, whether it's from your favourite song, the rhythmic wash of waves on the seashore, or an ancient musical instrument is one of the cheapest and easiest ways to access healing and to recover when life's hurdles knock us down.

MUSIC MAKES you feel less isolated and things like Spotify make it easy to choose the mood, and avoid repetitive sounds tracks.

IN 2019 I released the second book in my Transformational Super Kids series. It's called I Have to Grow. In this book, I share how Hannah was bullied as a child and told she couldn't sing.

Are bullies or self-doubt holding you back? Triumph over bullies! Discover how Hannah found her voice.

I Have to Grow is available in audiobook, hardcover, eBook and paper back from all online bookstores.

Sign up to my newsletter to learn when other books and audible versions, narrated by me, are released.

23

FEAR LESS

As author and filmmaker Michael Moore said, "I want us all to face our fears and stop behaving like our goal in life is merely to survive. Surviving is for game show contestants stranded in the jungle or on a desert island. You are not stranded. Use your power. You deserve better."

So many people let fear limit their potential. They fail before they even try. Fear of success, fear of failure, fear of disappointment, fear of humiliation, fear of losing your relationship—the list goes on.

There's a whole swag of fears out there and a host of industries clamouring to feed it. Cultivating fear is big business and the favoured official tool for control by oppressive totalitarian agencies and regimes.

Fearful thinking can balloon into anxiety, paranoia, and paralysis.

It takes energy to rise above fear. But you can bounce back. You can reclaim your power—you can pour your energy into people, things and situations that spark joy. You can avoid people and situations that feed your anxiety.

Or you can be a stone wall and just let fear bounce off you. Perhaps you may decide to face your fear and remind it you're the boss—what you say, what you want, what you desire goes. Full stop.

As Susan Jeffers, the author of *Feel the Fear and Do It Anyway* so eloquently advised, you can do the thing you fear and the death of fear is certain.

Or, as the Buddhist nun Pema Chodron advises, you can cultivate loving kindness toward your fear.

> "Openness doesn't come from resisting our fears but from getting to know them well. We can't cultivate fearlessness without compassionate inquiry into the workings of ego. So, we ask ourselves, 'What happens when I feel I can't handle what's going on? What are the stories I tell myself? What repels me and what attracts me? Where do I look for strength and in what do I place my trust?'"

Cultivate curiosity and consider asking your fear to have a chat with you. Ask, "Fear, what are you wanting to say?" "What do you want me to know?" "Fear, what are you wanting to teach me?" "How will you help me fulfil my highest potential?"

One of my fears is of living in poverty. Mystics have told me it's a fear that I have brought forward from past lives.

As a self-employed business owner who makes her living from creativity, I know that many artists are starving artists. But if I challenge my fear I am reminded that the opposite is also true.

The gift of this fear is the way it fires my determination to succeed. I don't want to fail, and I don't want to surround myself with people or situations that feed my fears.

One of the best ways to overcome this fear of being an impoverished artist is to learn from others who have succeeded. I study their books and oracles of wisdom, I listen to their podcasts and devour their wise words of success, and I pay it forward by sharing what I learn so that other people, like you, may succeed.

Conquering your fears and helping others do the same is a fabulous bounce strategy.

24

GO LOW

When life knocks you flat exercise self-compassion and give yourself permission to go low.

It's important to value less-than-positive feelings in equal measure—many times going low is an essential part of your healing process. Remind yourself that grief, loss and the disappointment you feel when you lose someone or something you love, are natural and valid emotions.

Similarly, when you suffer a setback it's natural to be hacked off, hurt or sad.

It's difficult to bounce back when you feel flat. But you must be true to yourself and allow your emotions to be felt and expressed, or risk them doing a sit-in, and being unwilling to budge.

The trick is not to stay low. Be watchful and know when a low mood has the potential to cross the threshold into clinical depression.

Your ability to bounce-back will only stay low if you hold it down and don't take proactive action to help elevate your mood. This may be simply talking to someone, sharing your emotions with a friend or a skilled professional like a counsellor, or allowing yourself some time to dress in black.

Sometimes, medical intervention may be required to help you cope with extreme and entrenched cases of low mood.

Practicing some of the other mood enhancing strategies in this book, or recalling a time where you felt similarly stuck and remembering the things that helped you bounce back, may also help you recover your vitality.

If you're worried that you may be clinically depressed don't be too proud to ask for help. You don't have to suffer alone.

All suffering will pass. Any darkness you feel engulfing you right now may just be the experience that will move you into a new authentic expression of your spirit. As day follows night, so will light come after a dark period of the soul.

25

LOOK FOR THE GIFT

Sometimes in life, as with photography, you need a negative to develop the positive. What at the time seemed like a low point can, with hindsight, prove to be the most life-changing and meaningful experience.

A classic and powerful bounce strategy is to reframe setbacks is to look for the treasures they may yield.

In *The Book of Joy,* two great spiritual teachers, the Dalai Lama, and Archbishop Desmond Tutu, men who have both known tremendous suffering, encourage us all to look for the gifts contained within adversity. One of these gifts is the opportunity to be reborn.

"When I spoke about mothers and childbirth, it seems to be a wonderful metaphor, actually, that nothing beautiful in the end comes without a measure of some pain, some frustration, some suffering," writes the Dalai Lama. "This is the nature of things. This is how our universe has been made up."

In the same book, the Dalai Lama shares how the gift of being exiled from his beloved Tibet provided the opportunity to give birth to a new way of being and to share his teachings and Buddhist philosophy throughout the world. "Life is suffering," he says. "It's how you react to life that changes your karma", he teaches. "I'm just one human being, but I believe each one of us has a responsibility to contribute to a happier humanity."

It is no coincidence that successful and revered people see the cup half full, look for ways to add more to peoples' lives rather than play the victim, and demand that life treats them more favourably.

"If I had been brought up protected and happy, what the devil would I write about?" says Isabel Allende of her troubled childhood. The gift of her previous unhappiness creates bounce in the lives of millions of readers who are enchanted by her words and are inspired by Allende's tales of passion, courage, endurance, and hope.

26

JOURNAL YOUR WAY TO JOY

In 2018, while tackling a mammoth writing project, I talked myself into a bit of a funk. I knew that what I really needed were some positive reminders of my intentions and a way to encourage perseverance.

I recalled a strategy Anne Gracie, a successful romance author, once shared in a newsletter, "I love my writing journal. It's my partner in writing, there for me whenever I need it, my confidant and my supporter and my record of where I've been."

Prior to this, I had noticed anxiety building—as it always does when I don't have a special book in which to purge and reshape my thoughts.

Instead of saying "I quit" and "I am so over this," and retelling the story that allowed for failure, I went online and purchased a beautiful unlined leather-bound sketchbook.

With my gold pen, I wrote empowering and encouraging quotes from other authors who have also struggled to maintain a prosperous mindset while writing an epic book.

Top of my list was Jessie Burton's empowering words, "Always picture succeeding, never let it fade. Always picture success, no matter how badly things seem to be going in the moment."

These words reminded me that I was picturing failure. I was

telling myself messages of failure. I was feeling like a failure.

Jesse Burton, the author of *The Muse and The Miniaturist*, is very inspiring to me because she is so honest about her own battles with mental health—including anxiety.

"In February, I was publicly honest about how difficult it had been to handle, process and assimilate in real time some of the changes in my life. Namely, the strange and wondrous effects of *The Miniaturist*. I wrote about anxiety, my first tentative foray into putting that mental morass into words," she wrote in one of her newsletters.

As Burton highlights, blogging and sharing your thoughts with your fans is another form of cathartic journaling—as is writing a book like this.

To minimise stress and boost your bounce mindset, another form of journaling is writing Morning Pages, a strategy developed by Julia Cameron, author of *The Artist's Way*.

The writing is just a stream of consciousness, writing out whatever you are feeling—good (or what one of my clients calls the "sunnies") or not so good ("the uglies").

"It's a way of clearing the mind—a farewell to what has been and a hello to what will be," Cameron says.

"Write down just what is crossing your consciousness. Cloud thoughts that move across consciousness. Meeting your shadow and taking it out for a cup of coffee so it doesn't eddy your consciousness during the day."

The point of this writing is to work with your subconscious and let it work its magic in the creative, healing process.

Keep a writing journal for specific writing projects. It may not work for you, but you will never know until you try.

Start where you are—commit to a daily practice of writing Morning Pages and journal for self-exploration.

Dive Deeper. . .

You can find out more about Morning Pages here http://juliacameronlive.com/basic-tools/morning-pages/

27

EXPRESS YOURSELF

Creative expression and communicating what you truly feel is one of our greatest freedoms. It a simple, joyful and effective way to inject more bounce in your life.

"I write songs to deal with things I otherwise might not be able to," a young woman once said about her budding music career, hobbies and dreams.

"For me to be happy is about pleasing only my heart and not worrying about what others think," says Interior designer Olimpia Orsini about her magically surreal lair in her home away from home in Rome's bohemian Campo Marzio.

"I love what a camera does," says landscape photographer Alicia Taylor. "It opens up people to connect with you, it can take you on an amazing journey, and probably is the only time I feel I've got the guts to do something is when I've got the camera in my hands. I feel like it's a key to the world."

"Knitting saved my life," the waitress at my local cafe told me recently. She told me how her hobby has provided the ultimate cure for her anxiety, and of the joy she finds in knitting for friends.

Without the anxiety of feeling different, author Isabel Allende, says she wouldn't have been driven to create. "Writing, when all is said and done, is an attempt to understand one's own circumstance and to clarify the confusion of existence, including insecurities that do not torment normal people, only chronic non-conformists."

What do these people all have in common? They harness the power of creative expression to rise above the challenges of life.

Don't get caught up in the classical definitions of an artist when you think about creativity, but you don't have to be an artist, painter or sculptor to be creative. Expressing your thoughts, or imagining what doesn't yet exist and then bringing it into being lies at the heart of creative expression.

You could harness the transformational power of creativity by:

• Imagining what could be
• Dreaming
• Challenging the status quo
• Generating ideas
• Designing new products or services
• Expressing thoughts and feelings that are too big or too difficult to put into words visually

Or doing something else that helps you deal with life and creates joy in your heart.

One of the most liberating features of the creative process is that it triggers moments of vitality and connection.

"The arts address the idea of an aesthetic experience.," says Ken Robinson, an internationally recognised leader in the development of creativity.

"An aesthetic experience is one in which the senses are operating at their peak, when you are present in the current moment, when you are resonating with the excitement of this thing that you are experiencing, when you are fully alive."

Being fully alive is part of the enchantment that creative expression holds. This transformational process connects you to your authentic self. But to free yourself you must act.

As Shakespeare once said, "Joy's soul lies in the doing."

28

MAKE MISTAKES

Conquering failure often requires learning the hard way to reach dizzying heights and allowing room for disappointment.

Julia Cameron, the author of *The Artist's Way*, advises aspiring authors to affirm the following, "I am willing to write badly; I am willing to do the work whether it is any good or not; I am also willing to allow brilliance." It's wisdom we can all embrace.

Many people stagnate under the weight of perfectionism or fear of failing because they worry about making mistakes.

It may be challenging, but investing in strategies to create more tolerance and acceptance towards making mistakes will prove liberating. One strategy is to learn from others' misfortune.

With hindsight, sometimes the greatest fortune comes from making the biggest blunders. Here are just a few mistakes that turned out well:

Isabel Allende started her career in journalism and soon found herself offside with people who didn't appreciate her outspoken views. For years she felt under-appreciated—until she decided to tackle her first novel, *The House of the Spirits*.

The novel was named Best Novel of the Year in Chile in 1982, and Allende received the country's Panorama Literario award. *The House of the Spirits* has been translated into more than 37 languages. It was also adapted into a film of the same name starring Jeremy Irons, Meryl Streep, Winona Ryder, Glenn Close, and Antonio Banderas.

Musician Ornette Coleman's mistake led her to be acclaimed as the inventor of "free jazz." She was awarded the MacArthur Fellowship (nicknamed the Genius Award) in 1994 and the Pulitzer Prize for Music in 2007.

"It was when I found out I could make mistakes that I knew I was on to something," she once said.

Walt Disney was fired by a newspaper for lack of ideas. He also went bankrupt several times before he and his brother co-founded Walt Disney Productions, one of the best-known motion picture production companies in the world. Disney's revenue last year was $US45 billion.

Dr. Suess' first children's book, *And to Think That I Saw it on Mulberry Street,* was rejected by 27 publishers. The 28th publisher, Vanguard Press, sold six million copies of the book. He went on to write numerous other books which still sell well today.

Rhonda Byrne's life was at an all-time low. Fifty-five and twice divorced, her father had just died and her career was in crisis.

That was until, acting on an inspired thought, she created the DVD *The Secret* and later produced a book, both of which galloped away to become some of the biggest-selling self-help resources of all time.

At the heart of Byrnes' inspirational series of products is the Law of Attraction.

"Everything in your life is attracted to you by what you are thinking," Rhonda says. "You are like a human transmission tower, transmitting a frequency with your thoughts. If you want to change anything in your life, change the frequency by changing your thoughts."

Refuse to be a victim. Next time you feel you've made a mistake, ask yourself, "How could this work out for my highest good?"

Be gentle with yourself. Sometimes making mistakes heralds a time of new birth and energy. Draw on the lessons you have learned to help you move forward

Notice how you have grown and changed due to everything that has happened. Gather information as you go and be ready for a new adventure. Look for positive signs for successful outcomes in the future.

Buoy your courage and resolve by collecting stories about other people who felt like failures, or were treated harshly by peers, critics, family, and other disbelievers. Collect a file of inspiring stories about mistakes that turned out well.

Follow your inspiration and bounce back from mistakes.

29

CHASE THE LIGHT

What's your default position when things go awry, obstacles challenge your resolve, technology goes belly-up, unforeseen demands on your time derail your plans, or you receive negative feedback?

Does your mood darken? Setbacks are normal foes that you'll meet on the path to success, but how you greet them will determine the outcome.

Keep your thoughts light. You may need to bring out the big guns to wage war against doubt, despair, and other dark, heavy thoughts.

While they're often part of the journey to success, you will need to slay them to stay motivated and optimistic.

Resilient people turn again and again toward the things that create light. They don't ignore the shadows, but they don't allow their mindset to be overloaded by darkness.

Acceptance, optimism, willpower, grit, stubborn determination, and a resolve to persevere are critical skills to cultivate, as is flexibility and the willingness to adapt.

Sometimes when it's all too hard and you need to hibernate, you may temporarily quit. You can take a lesson from nature in this regard.

But as sure as night follows day, and the seasons have their rhythm, if writing is your gift, your purpose, the thing that makes you happy, before long you'll be up and writing again.

Resist complaining and victim talk—it increases toxicity in your mind and body, hampering your progress.

Throw your energy into positivity—strive to engineer and implement solutions, no matter how small.

30

CONFLICT HAPPENS

As much as we all like to get on, sometimes conflict is inevitable.

People may feel threatened by your success, they may deliberately try to thwart you, or they may misunderstand your motives and desires.

Your family and loved ones may resent the time you need to spend away from them. You may feel guilty for wanting more from your life.

As da Vinci said, the noblest pleasure is the joy of understanding. Seek first to understand, and then plan your conflict-handling strategy.

This is a message that British architect Dame Zaha Mohammad Hadid took to heart. "Women are always told, 'You're not going to make it, it's too difficult, you can't do that, don't enter this competition, you'll never win it.' They need confidence in themselves and people around them to help them to get on," she once said.

"Unless you're prepared to die for your work, you're no good," she once said. Hadid was a phenomenal architect, and, in 2004, was the first woman to receive the Pritzker Architecture Prize.

However, Hadid's success wasn't achieved without criticism. Her bounce strategy was to remain true to her vision and do what she believed.

Fight for your dreams and sharpen your conflict resolution skills so you can bounce back if people go on the attack.

31

RELATIONSHIP BOUNCE

In a universe where "like goes to like" and "birds of a feather flock together," we attract to us that which we emanate.

Everything connects to everything else, especially when it comes to the health of your relationships.

Leonardo da Vinci once said, "Marriage is like putting your hand into a bag of snakes in the hope of pulling out an eel."

Read into this what you will, but the theme is clear. Make good choices and marry well, keep your relationship in good health, or don't marry at all.

Bounce relationships that are dragging you down. Sometimes this means investing more time and energy into making things work, or having a bit more patience when people important to you aren't at their best. Take the good with the bad, don't give up too easily, work at it and recognise that nothing is absolutely perfect.

If people try to pull you down, take a step back and explore their motives. Fear is often the culprit. The fear that you may surpass them. The fear that your success will highlight their own regrets. Or the fear that when you succeed you will leave them.

If you can't make things work, professionally or personally, be prepared to quit. Divorce your job, your boss, your partner—anyone who is toxic to your health and happiness.

Getting your head bitten off, or feeling like you're surrounded by a vat of snakes, or being held down, will only deflate your ability to bounce.

32

BOUNCE AWAY FROM YOUR ENVIRONMENT

Consider where you are working, where you are living, who you are associating with and how these environmental factors are either strengthening you or holding you back.

Sometimes you need to bounce away to a more liberating and supportive environment.

A great number of people, by choice or by fate have forged a successful path after leaving their environment. His Holiness the Dalai Lama was forced to flee Tibet following the invasion by the Chinese.

"Suffering is inevitable," he said, "But how we respond to that suffering is our choice. Not even oppression or occupation can take away this freedom to choose our response."

Rather than become angry, depressed or flat the Dalai Lama found strength in his spiritual practices and philosophy. There is a *Sutta*, or teaching of the Buddha, called the *Sallatha Sutta*, that makes a similar distinction between 'feelings of pain' and 'the suffering that comes as a result of our response' to pain. Or to put more simply, pain is inevitable and suffering is optional.

"There are different aspects to any event. For example, we lost our own country and became refugees, but that same experience gave us new opportunities to see more things. For me personally, I had more opportunities to meet with different people, different spiritual practitioners, like you, and also scientists. This new opportunity arrived because I became a refugee," he writes in *The Book of Joy*.

"If I remained in the Potala in Lhasa, I would have stayed in what has often been described as a golden cage: The Lama, holy Dalai Lama. So, personally, I prefer the last five decades of refugee life. It's more useful, more opportunity to learn, to experience life. Therefore, if you look from one angle, you feel, oh how bad, how sad. But if you look from another angle at that same tragedy, that same event, you see that it gives me new opportunities. So, it's wonderful. That's the main reason that I'm not sad and morose. There's a Tibetan saying: 'Wherever you have friends that's your country, and wherever you receive love, that's your home.'"

Home, they say, is where your heart is. If your current situation isn't sparking joy, or is impacting your health, leap away. Commit to finding your soul space.

Whether by force or by choice, a new house, a new town, a new country may just be the change of scene you need.

33

BOUNCEY WORK

What you do for a living plays a major role in your happiness and wellbeing. When you do what you love, work doesn't feel like a chore at all. If you plan it well, your chosen vocation can feel like a vacation and wash away the dust of everyday life.

The opposite is also true.

If Monday mornings are a low point in your week, it may be a sign that it's time for a new career. And you're not alone. Research shows that less than 10% of people are visibly living their passion.

Career dissatisfaction, aching boredom, and gnawing unfulfilment are common causes of stress, low productivity, poor performance and plummeting levels of confidence and self-esteem.

To find a job you truly love an easy place to start is to use current things getting you down as signposts to your preferred future. Confirming what's causing your job blues will put more bounce into your career and help you get clear about your intentions, options, and possibilities.

Another great strategy is spending more time getting to know you, getting clear about who you are and what you need to feel happy and fulfilled. You'll then be better able to bounce toward a new career.

What are your bounce factors? What makes you jump for joy? If you want to feel happy in your job you need to be clear about all the things that make you feel passionate and alive.

Some things to consider include:

- Your core values, beliefs, and deepest interests
- Your strengths, gifts, and talents, you love doing
- The sort of work environment that best suits you
- What sort of people you want to work with
- Your personality and what makes you tick
- The things that give your life meaning and purpose
- What you love!

"There is no mistaking love. You feel it in your heart. It is the common fibre of life, the flame that heals our soul, energises our spirit and supplies passion to our lives," says psychiatrist, Elizabeth Kubler-Ross. Don't give up until you've found the things that ignite your soul.

You'll find plenty of inspiration and practical strategies in my *Mid-life Career Rescue* series, and *How to Find Your Passion and Purpose* and also my online course *Follow Your Passion to Prosperity*.

34

MAGIC MORNINGS

"If you win the morning, you win the day," says millionaire author, podcaster and polymath Tim Ferriss. Despite his phenomenal success Tim suffers from anxiety and credits a robust morning routine and other health behaviours with giving him more bounce throughout the day.

Ferriss kick-starts his day with 10-20 minutes of transcendental meditation, five to 10 minutes of journaling or Morning Pages, making his bed, and a healthy dose of positive vibes. He also does at least 30 seconds of light exercise. 30 seconds!

"Getting into my body, even for 30 seconds, has a dramatic effect on my mood and quiets mental chatter," Ferriss wrote in his book *Tools of Titans.*

I've followed a similar ritual for years—long before I discovered Tim Ferris. But whenever I am tempted to flag my meditation or my ritual of writing in my journal, I find it helpful to remind myself these are the tools Titans like Tim use to achieve phenomenal results.

Below are just a few of the many *Magic Morning* routines and rituals you can use to prime your day for miracles:

• Meditation and mindfulness—enjoy some sacred silence

• Affirmations—empower your beliefs with feeling-based reminders of your intentions

• Goals to go for—set your priorities, including health and well-being activities (exercise, etc.)

• Inspiration—journaling, visualisation, reading

• Co-create—partner with spirit, tap into your Higher Self, evoke the muse...and get ready to create

Importantly, complete these crucial focusing activities *before* you get to work.

I experience many of these activities simultaneously when I meditate, write my Morning Pages, and consult the oracles; and also when I go for a walk in nature, listen to an uplifting audiobook or podcast, or sip my morning coffee.

Ferriss, in a podcast episode, sums up the potency of similar mindful practices: "It's easy to become obsessed with pushing the ball forward as a Type-A personality and end up a perfectionist who is always future-focused.

"The five-minute journal is a therapeutic intervention, for me at least, because I am that person. That allows me to not only get more done during the day but to also feel better throughout the entire day, to be a happier person, to be a more content person—which is not something that comes naturally to me."

I'm not alone in knowing the positive difference daily habits like journaling or taking the time to reconnect with my higher self, makes to my resilience and happiness levels.

Get your day off to a high-vibration start. Choose, develop, and apply your own Magic Morning routines.

35

CONSULT THE ORACLES

Another morning ritual I love is beginning my day being intuitively guided by oracle cards. Not everyone believes in mysticism—but I do. And so do a great many others.

"If you want to be a serious writer or intellectual you can't say you're a mystic because no one will talk to you again," says American author (and professional tarot card reader) Jessa Crispin, slightly tongue-in-cheek.

But, it may surprise you to know that many Titans consult oracles to improve their mindset and boost their productivity and performance.

Subjects such as astrology, psychic phenomena, spirituality, and a fascination with tarot and oracle cards have helped many creative people and successful entrepreneurs overcome doubt, strengthen their beliefs, clarify their direction and find meaning in challenging situations.

As I share in my book *The Art of Success: How Extraordinary Artists Can Help You Succeed in Business and Life,* Coco Chanel found great wisdom, peace, comfort, and healing from oracle cards and an eclectic array of spiritual rituals.

Oracle reader and spiritual adviser, Colette Barron-Reid credits this spiritual practice, and others, with saving her life and helping her recover from chronic alcoholism and drug abuse.

"Faith in the guidance of Spirit gives you the courage to take risks because you're assured that whatever happens, a Higher Power is on your side and you will survive," says Barron-Reid.

"Increasing numbers of people are looking to ancient oracles to receive personal guidance because they are not getting the answers and insights they need when they consult the usual sources of psychology and science," she says.

However, there are some highly influential psychologists who do value the wisdom and intuitive guidance that oracles herald.

Of all the psychological theories in the West, that of revered Swiss psychologist Carl Jung stands out as most applicable.

Jung wrote about Tarot on several occasions, seeing it as depicting archetypes of transformation like those he found in myths, dreams, and alchemy.

He described its divinatory abilities as similar to the ancient divination text I Ching, and to astrology. Later in life, Jung established a group which attempted to integrate insights about a person based on multiple divination systems including Tarot.

Jung, Crispin, Colette Barron-Reid, and other healers like myself are proud to join many others who invite people to experience a new, or rather an old way, of finding hope, courage, and comfort to live an inspired, joyful life.

Consider experimenting with oracles and making these, and other spiritual practices, part of your daily bounce ritual.

36

FAITH IN YOUR STARS

"Most clients come with financial problems or relationship problems," my friend and astrologer Marianne O'Hagan says. "They come looking for the hope of happiness in the future."

Marianne knows personally and professionally how astrology can help during times of stress and worry. You can read more of her story in *Mid-Life Career Rescue: What Makes You Happy*—including how she started her own business by using her faith in the stars.

"I liked the idea that astrology believes we all are special and have unique gifts. It was at that moment that my love of astrology was born," she says.

As Pam Gregory shares in her fabulous book, *How to Co-Create using the Secret Language of the Universe: Using Astrology for your Empowerment*, many eminent psychologists, including Carl Jung, regard astrology as sacred science. Jung used astrological insights to help diagnose his patients, and as inspiration for his psychological theories of synchronicity and archetypes.

Knowing who you are and what makes you tick, and what doesn't, is truly an empowering and life-changing experience. 'Know thyself' is a maxim that is as true now as it was in ancient times.

I'm a Libra in Western astrology and a Snake in Chinese astrology.

It's true when they say that Librans love harmony, balance, and beauty. I love it when I receive feedback from readers, saying my book is "beautifully written."

Or, as one person who posted in their review of my first *Art of Success* book, inspired by Leonardo da Vinci, posted in their review, "*This beautiful book wraps art around business and life and makes each hum with energy and creativity and brings the reader new vitality.*"

Google 'best careers' for Snakes and I'm told to avoid careers where I have to work too hard. 'Working hard' to me is doing something I dislike, working with people I don't respect. Working hard is not marching to my own beat. But when I'm working in the passion zone, fulfilling my purpose, now that's a different story.

Whether or not you're a believer in the notion that whatever planets align at the time and place of your birth, can determine your intrinsic strengths, shape your character, relationships and fortunes, there's plenty of helpful data to aid you in your quest for success. Keep an open mind and don't take everything as total gospel.

Go cosmic—gain additional insight about your astrological sign from any of the plethora of books, online resources, and personal astrologers. Focus on identifying your strengths, Achilles heel, and best-fit-factors career-wise and in your personal life.

37

MINDFUL MEDITATION

Our brains never get a break and the results can be increased stress, anxiety, insomnia and if left unchecked, even depression. But there is something you can do—meditate.

Meditation changes brain patterns, soothes and connects you to your Higher Self. It's one of the most powerful bounce strategies you'll ever discover.

"It's the Swiss army knife of medical tools, for conditions both small and large," writes Arianna Huffington, the founder of *The Huffington Post* and author of *Thrive*.

So, what's the buzz? Recent research published in *New Scientist* has revealed that meditation can help to calm people and reduce fear. The research found that regular meditation can tame the amygdala, an area of the brain which is the hub of fear memory.

People who meditate regularly are less likely to be shocked, flustered, surprised, or as angry as other people, and have a greater stress tolerance threshold as a result.

By meditating regularly, the brain is reoriented from a stressful fight-or-flight response to one of acceptance, a shift that increases contentment, enthusiasm, and feelings of happiness. Here are a few of the many ways a regular meditative practice will help you bounce:

- Decreased stress and anxiety
- Improved focus, memory, and learning ability
- Heightened recharging capacity
- Higher IQ and more efficient brain functioning
- Increased blood circulation and reduced hyperactivity in the brain, slower wavelengths and decreased beta waves (Beta State:13—30Hz) means more time between thoughts which leads to more skilful decision making
- Increased Theta State (4—8Hz) and Delta States (1—3 Hz) which deepens awareness and strengthens intuition and visualisation skills
- Increased creativity and connection with your higher intelligence

When Tim Ferriss, who practices transcendental meditation, sat down with more than 200 people at the height of their field for his new book, *Tools of Titans*, he found that 80% followed some form of guided mindfulness practice.

It took Ferriss a while to get into meditation, he says in a podcast episode about his own morning routine. But since he discovered that the majority of world-class performers meditated, he also decided to follow the habit.

His practice takes up 21 minutes a day: one minute to get settled and 20 minutes to meditate.

Ferriss recommends two apps for those wanting some help getting started—*Headspace* or *Calm*.

"Start small, rig the game so you can win it, get in five sessions before you get too ambitious with length," says Ferriss.

"You have to win those early sessions so you establish it as a habit, so you don't have the cognitive fatigue of that practice."

Many people find that meditating for 20 minutes in the morning and 20 minutes at the end of the day yields remarkable benefits.

Regularly take time to focus on the present moment. Make meditating for at least 20 minutes a day part of your daily routine for optimum success and well-being.

38

SLEEP

Are you getting enough sleep? It's hard to bounce if you're sleep deprived and your energy is flat.

"We're suffering a sleep crisis," warns Arianna Huffington, co-founder and editor-in-chief of *The Huffington Post* and author of *The Sleep Revolution: Transforming Your Life One Night at a Time*.

Modern science proves conclusively that if you skip out on sleep you're compromising not just your productivity and efficiency, but also your health and wellbeing.

More than a third of American adults are not getting enough sleep on a regular basis, according to a February 2016 study from the Centers for Disease Control and Prevention.

Sleeping less than seven hours a day, they report, can lead to an increased risk of frequent mental distress, impaired thinking, reduced cognitive ability, and increased susceptibility to depression.

Lack of sleep also increases the likelihood of obesity, diabetes, high blood pressure, heart disease, and stroke. None of which will aid your quest for happiness and joy.

Getting enough quality sleep helps you maintain your mental and physical health and enhances your quality of life. Getting enough shuteye helps you keep the world in perspective, and enables you to refocus on the essence of who you are. In that place of connection, it's easier for the fears and concerns of the world to drop away.

The next time you're worrying and feeling anxious around bedtime, try one of these simple hacks to relax and quieten your mind enough to fall asleep:

- Enjoy a calming cup of herbal tea
- Listen to soothing music
- Read a paperback novel or book of poems
- Take an aromatherapy bath with lavender and other scented oils
- Or, spend time enjoying your favourite relaxation or meditation practice.

You can also enhance your sleep by turning off all devices at least an hour before you go to bed leaving them outside your bedroom.

If lack of sleep is keeping you awake at night and making you tired during the day, consider reading and applying the strategies in Arianna Huffington's book, *The Sleep Revolution: Transforming Your Life One Night at a Time*.

Be ruthless about prioritising your well-being. Remind yourself of the benefits that will flow when you enhance the length and quality of your sleep.

39

UNPLUG

Are you permanently attached to your device? Are you suffering from information overwhelm? Does the thought of unplugging from technology send your anxiety spiralling?

What if you miss something? What if....what if...What if you shut it all down and stepped away for a day, a week, a month, or more?

Setting aside protected time each day for direct interaction with people—or for solitude and meditation without scrolling through social media feeds, or fielding a stream of texts—instinctively feels like a good thing, but it's not always easy.

Take time out to unplug, take a step back, forget about what is expected, forget about what you may be missing, and think about what you may be gaining.

Besides the main benefit of being able to enjoy much more peace and hassle-free, uninterrupted time, here are seven other wonderful and lesser-known upsides you'll notice from making the decision to unplug regularly:

Enhanced relationships. Disconnecting from your perpetual tether to iPhones and laptops can do wonders for your real-world connections. This is a no-brainer and one that so many people seem to miss. Putting your device away and giving the people around you your undivided attention, rather than your device, tells your family, friends and loved ones that they're important to you.

Increased awareness. When was the last time you were fully aware of the beauty that surrounds you? When you unplug, you blitz major distractions. You become aware of small details in people, things, and places that you never really noticed before.

Clarity. Unplugging reduces brain overload. Technological over-stimulation overwhelms your mind, reducing your cognitive reasoning skills.

Improved memory retention and mood. Even just detoxing from technology for one day per week is enough to reboot your brain, which can improve your memory and lift your mood—giving you more bounce.

More brain power. Spending less time being a slave to technological stimulation provides time to focus on activities that grow your brain cells. Engaging an enjoyable hobby, learning a new skill, visiting a new place, having new experiences, or going for a relaxing walk.

Enhanced productivity. Do you really need constant access to your social media notifications, your email inbox, a bunch of tabs open in your web browser and other online distractions, to feel in touch and in control?

Accumulating interruptions steals your peace of mind and minimises your ability to get things done. Any time you're interrupted from a work-related task by devices, it can take as long as 45 minutes for your brain to refocus.

Mindfulness. When something interesting starts happening, what's your first reaction? Do you whip out your phone, start snapping photos and begin sharing on social media? Or do you savour the moment and delight in being present in that moment? When you unplug, you force yourself to be more present.

Get to the heart of why you're spending so much time connected to technology. Isolate the benefits and issues, and then make a decision whether you need to schedule the time to unplug.

40

AVOID OVER-STIMULATION

Sometimes the best way to bounce is to eat what you don't want, drink what you don't like, and do what you'd rather avoid.

Knock things like coffee, caffeinated drinks and foods, alcohol, and nicotine off your list (or at least limit your intake).

These trigger the production of the stress-related hormone adrenaline—which increases your heart rate, prompts the liver to release more sugar into your bloodstream, and makes the lungs take in more oxygen.

While these things may give you a short-term high, in the long run, the result is fatigue and low energy levels. This, in turn, leads to a vicious cycle of relying on more stimulants to get you through the day.

The impact of excessive coffee and caffeinated drinks has become such a health hazard, a new disorder, Caffeine Use Disorder, was recently added to the DSM-V—the tool psychologists, psychiatrists, and other mental health professionals often refer to prior to making their diagnosis.

Are you addicted to caffeine?

If you've experienced these three symptoms within the past year —you may be in trouble:

• You have a persistent desire to give up or cut down on caffeine use, or you've tried to do so unsuccessfully.
• You continue to use caffeine despite knowing it contributes to recurring physical or psychological problems for you (like insomnia, or jitteriness).
• You experience withdrawal symptoms if you don't have your usual amount of caffeine.

Many of my clients notice reduced levels of anxiety, irritability, and depression when they kick the habit. They also report feeling better able to cope with stress, once the coffee habit is culled.

Opt for a natural high. Consider replacing caffeine, alcohol, nicotine and other stimulants with fresh juices, exercise, meditation, or some other activity which makes you feel great and sustains energy. Herbal teas are also healthy caffeine-free alternatives. Try to drink 6-8 glasses (1.7-2 liters) of water a day to boost energy and flush out toxins.

Less artificial stimulation means more natural life-affirming highs.

41

MOOD FOOD

As I shared in my book *Developing a Millionaire Mindset* successful people make their health a priority and regularly tune into their body barometers.

It's tougher to bounce if you lack energy, feel stressed, sluggish, lethargic, or unhealthy. Artificially stimulating your mind, body, and soul won't cut it in the long term.

Many of us take for granted how magnificent and clever our bodies are. But for everything to fire optimally, you need to fuel it with food geared for performance, eat mindfully, and not inhale your meal in a race to the finish.

You are what you feed your stomach—which also feeds your mind. For optimum performance, ensure you're putting smart fuel into your body.

Modern nutritionists and health professionals warn of the perils of over- and under-eating; not eating fresh, seasonal, organic food; and chewing insufficiently.

Diabetes is on the rise. Obesity is an epidemic. Cholesterol and blood pressure are going through the roof. And stress, depression, anxiety, and other mental troubles are all trending upward.

Your gut is also your second brain—a major receptor site of

dopamine, a neurotransmitter that helps control the brain's reward and pleasure centres.

Dopamine helps regulate the feel-good emotions we all need to fuel success. It also regulates movement—enabling you to not only see the rewards of your efforts but to also take action towards them.

Benefits of healthy eating practices include:

• Increased clarity of thinking
• Better memory
• Healthy body weight
• Increased positive emotions
• Enhanced mental, emotional, and physical health
• Improved mood
• More energy and stamina
• Increased goal achievement
• Better sleep
• Longevity

Avoid extremes—too much sloth makes one prone to gluttony, too much activity overwhelms, and too many vain pleasures taken to extremes are a cause of failure.

As I've already highlighted, too much coffee, for example, increases feelings of anxiety. Too much booze, as you'll discover in the next chapter, can send your stress levels soaring.

When you switch from eating unhealthily to healthily, the difference will be tangibly transformative.

Don't forget to set your self up for a bouncy day by eating a nourishing breakfast. Too many people skip this important start to the day.

At first glance, **porridge** might not seem like the most exciting breakfast on the planet. But it's great for your health and way better than a greasy fry-up. One bowl of porridge contains more fibre than a slice of wholemeal bread and is rich in minerals including copper, iron. and manganese.

It's also been proven to prevent blood sugar spikes, due to the low glycemic index of oats.

Listed below are some helpful energy-enhancing, mood boosting food tips:

• Eat small but regular meals to sustain energy levels and keep blood sugar levels steady
• Meat and fish contain beneficial amounts of iron, as do green leafy vegetables, dried apricots, lentils and other pulses
• Make sure you get sufficient amounts of B-group vitamins, particularly riboflavin, which converts carbohydrates into energy; vitamin B6 essential for energy metabolism; and vitamin B12, required for forming red blood cells that carry oxygen throughout the body. Useful sources of B-group vitamins include whole-grains, chicken, fish, eggs, dairy produce, pulses, shellfish and red meat
• Help your body absorb more iron by drinking a glass of orange juice once a day with a meal. Vitamin C also helps to boost energy
• Other vital minerals include magnesium, which works with potassium and sodium to ensure the efficient working of muscles, along with zinc, which protects against viral infections that often precede chronic fatigue

Avoid

• Sugary foods, including biscuits, cakes, and chocolate. These also promote short-term energy highs, leading to irritability and lethargy
• Alcohol in large quantities
• Refined carbohydrates foods like white bread, pasta, and rice. These destabilise energy levels by causing a sharp increase in blood sugar levels

It's easy to miss meals when you're busy, or stressed, so plan ahead. Your body, mind and spirit will love you back.

42

MINDFUL DRINKING

Many people mistakenly believe drinking alcohol will increase their happiness. But alcohol is a depressant and in large quantities is draining on your body and mind.

Experience may have already taught you that too much booze muddles the mind, ignites aggression, reduces responsiveness, and ultimately depresses.

It's also hard to quit—alcohol is one of the most addictive legal drugs on the planet.

It's also a well-documented neurotoxin—a toxic substance that inhibits, damages, and destroys the tissues of your nervous system.

To bounce, many people limit their drinking or consciously decide not to touch a drop. Keeping their resolve often takes extraordinary willpower.

Author and public speaker Deepak Chopra gave up drinking. "I liked it too much," he once said. Steven King, after almost losing his family and destroying his writing career, managed to quit.

Other people like Amy Winehouse devastatingly never made it. At only 27, she died of alcohol poisoning in 2011.

The risk of suicide also increases for stressed workers who turn to drink. As I've already discussed, alcohol abuse and excessive drinking is a major cause of anxiety and depression, impairs mental reasoning and critical thinking—increasing the likelihood of making tragic and often impulsive choices.

Risking destroying your career, ruining your relationships, sacrificing your sanity, and in the extreme, taking your life, is a massive price to pay for a mistaken belief that to be happy, or to numb your anxiety or cope with stress you need to drink more booze.

Bounce beautifully by exploring your relationship to drink and approaching it more mindfully. Consider, a period of sobriety. Instead of focusing on what you may be giving up, turn your mind to what you may gain—a better, more energised version of yourself.

The many benefits of reducing your alcohol intake, or not drinking at all, include:

✓ A stronger ability to focus on your goals and dreams
✓ Improved confidence and self-esteem
✓ Increased productivity
✓ Increased memory, mental performance, and decision-making
✓ Better control of your emotions
✓ Sweeter relationships
✓ Greater intuition and spiritual intelligence
✓ Authentic happiness

Not everyone battles with booze. Whether you cut back or eliminate alcohol entirely, the choice is ultimately yours. Only you know the benefits alcohol delivers or the success it destroys.

If you'd like to experiment with a period of sobriety or you need help to you moderate your drinking, *Mind Your Drink: The Surprising Joy of Sobriety*, available as a paperback and eBook will help.

You can also find a range of books and resources offering help to quit, including alcohol-free alternatives on my website—http://www.cassandragaisford.com/books-and-resources/control-alcohol/

43

YOGA

Yoga, relaxation, and mindfulness practices work behind-the-scenes to help lower the stress hormone cortisol.

Just two 90-minute classes a week is enough to notice an improved stress response, even in those who report being highly distressed, according to research on yoga and meditation coming out of Germany. Study participants noted a decrease in stress, anxiety, and depression.

I came across the following quote, source unknown, and it seems to summarise the key benefits of yoga—flexibility...in body, mind, and spirit: "Blessed are the flexible, for they shall not be bent out of shape."

Yoga classes don't have to be difficult. They can vary from gentle and soothing, to strenuous and challenging; the choice of style tends to be based on personal preference and physical ability.

Hatha yoga is the most common type of yoga practiced in the United States and combines three elements: physical poses, called *asanas*; controlled breathing practiced in conjunction with asanas; and a short period of deep relaxation or meditation.

"Available reviews of a wide range of yoga practices suggest they can reduce the impact of exaggerated stress responses and may be helpful for both anxiety and depression. In this respect, yoga functions like other self-soothing techniques, such as meditation, relaxation, exercise, or even socialising with friends," says an article posted by Harvard Medical School.

"By reducing perceived stress and anxiety, yoga appears to modulate stress response systems. This, in turn, decreases physiological arousal — for example, reducing the heart rate, lowering blood pressure, and easing respiration. There is also evidence that yoga practices help increase heart rate variability, an indicator of the body's ability to respond to stress more flexibly."

Researchers at the Walter Reed Army Medical Center in Washington, D.C., are offering a yogic method of deep relaxation to veterans returning from combat in Iraq and Afghanistan. Dr. Kristie Gore, a psychologist at Walter Reed, says the military hopes that yoga-based treatments will be more acceptable to the soldiers and less stigmatising than traditional psychotherapy. The centre now uses yoga and yogic relaxation in post-deployment PTSD awareness courses and plans to conduct a controlled trial of their effectiveness in the future.

Here are a few of the many reported benefits of yoga:

- Improvements in perceived stress, depression, anxiety, energy, fatigue, and well-being
- Reduced tension, anger, and hostility
- Reduced headaches and back pain
- Improved sleep quality
- Improved breathing and deeper relaxation

"*Samskara saksat karanat purvajati jnanam.* Through sustained focus and meditation on our patterns, habits, and conditioning, we gain knowledge and understanding of our past and how we can change the patterns that aren't serving us to live more freely and fully." ~ Yoga Sutra III.

Nurture your body and soul with regular yoga sessions.

44

BREATHE DEEPLY

In a state of joy and relaxation, you breathe in a deep circular pattern, your heart comes into coherence, and you begin to produce alpha brain waves, giving you access to your own natural tranquillisers and antidepressants.

But under stress your breathing is reversed. Instead of breathing slowly and deeply, your breathing tends to become shallower and more rapid. During times of extreme stress, you can forget to breathe at all!

You may even hyperventilate—breathing in an abnormally rapid, deep, or shallow pattern. You will exhale too much carbon dioxide, and as the level of carbon dioxide in the blood drops, the blood vessels narrow, allowing less blood to circulate. If too little blood reaches your brain, you'll become dizzy and may faint.

Calcium in the blood also decreases, causing some muscles and nerves to twitch. The twitching may result in a tingling or stabbing sensation near your mouth or in your chest. These symptoms include a tight feeling in the chest, as though your lungs cannot receive enough air.

This sensation leads to faster and deeper breathing. The heart may begin to pound, and the pulse rate may rise. Experiencing these symptoms will increase anxiety in some people, which can make the condition worse.

If this happens to you, or you have forgotten how to breathe, try this: breathe in deeply for a count of four, and exhale—slowing for a count of eight. Repeat 10 times. Notice how quickly your body and mind relax. Try this anywhere, anytime you notice feelings of stress returning, and beat the stress response. Or tap into a meditation or yoga class for enhanced breathing practice with the added benefit of a mind-body makeover.

Remember to breathe! Breathing deeply can evoke a state of calm and perspective during times of stress, allowing you to cope more effectively and bounce back from setbacks

45

GET OUTSIDE

It's hard to bounce when you're suffering from low mood. Very often a lack of outside time is the culprit. You're like a flower—you need at least 20 minutes of sunlight every day just to make your hormones work effectively and enable you to blossom to your fullest potential.

To feel and behave normally you need to be exposed to full-spectrum daylight on a regular basis. Medical research suggests some people need as much as two hours a day of sunlight to avoid Seasonal Affective Disorder.

Combine outside time with exercise like walking and not only will you get the light you need, but you'll also recharge your batteries.

Walking outside can also help you gain a new perspective on a troubling situation. When you go outside and take a walk, you increase the electrical activity in your brain, and you breathe negative ions and see in three dimensions.

All this helps you see with fresh eyes the things which are worrying you. Often you'll find that things are not as bad as they first appear, or discover a relatively simple solution.

Monitor how much time you spend indoors. Bounce away from habits that so many people have, like spending too many hours inside in front of two-dimensional computer monitors and TV screens, and then topping off a 12-hour day at work by trying to read themselves to sleep on their Kindle. These are all two-dimensional visual activities, which seldom spark joy.

Let mother earth, the sea, and the infinite sky boost your mood. Get outside and allow the sun and outside energy to lift your spirits. Schedule regular fresh air time. Improve your breathing, and take a brisk walk to increase your oxygen levels.

46

MOVE!

Many people lead sedentary lives, but the most successful ones praise the benefits of exercise. Many use their exercise as a time to reset and plan.

Vitamin D sufficiency, along with diet and exercise, has emerged as one of the most important success factors in human health.

During times of low mood, or high stress, you can become lethargic. Convincing yourself that you don't even have the energy or time to exercise can increase feelings of depression and irritability.

Discipline yourself to go out and get some fresh air—ideally somewhere not too frenzied.

Combine brisk walking with deep breathing to boost your energy levels, short-term memory, and state of mind.

When your breathing is calm and steady, your body is in a nurtured state which helps strengthen your immune system. This will help you ward off colds and snuffles.

Numerous studies have shown that exercise promotes the production of positive endorphins, which play a key role in making you feel better about yourself and your capacity to cope.

In the one-sided state of depression, there is very little electrical activity in the brain. A person on a stationary bike has more electrical activity in their brain than a person watching an educational video. The truly depressed person will have such low electrical activity that making basic decisions, including the mood-enhancing decision to exercise (even just a little), becomes very difficult.

Researchers also confirm there is a strong link between breathing, outside energy, and beneficial brainwave patterns. This may explain why so many people say that walking is their meditation—clearing their minds, and allowing space for good ideas to flourish.

Getting up and moving, embracing the flow of 'chi' in your entire system will enable you to activate both hemispheres of your brain – bringing a new perspective as well as a greater tolerance to life's stressors.

"It's not that I am thinking but I am in a kind of trance, totally connected with the present moment," Paulo Coelho says. When he returns to his work, his mind is clear and he is more powerfully connected to source energy.

Listen to your body barometer when it tells you to exercise more and sloth less.

Commit to a regular exercise regime and a healthier diet. Be consistent so that changes easily fall into place and become life-affirming habits.

47

THE BALANCED LIFE

Research proves that people who organize their whole life around their work are more prone to develop Post-Traumatic Embitterment Disorder—a disorder that covers almost every negative emotion a person can have at work.

On a typical day in the brain, trillions of messages are sent and received. The messages that are happy, upbeat messages are carried by the brain's 'happy messengers' (scientifically known as the Biogenic Amine/Endorphin System). Other messages are somber and disquieting. They are carried by the brain's 'sad messengers.'

Most nerve centres receive input from both types of messengers. So long as this input is balanced, everything runs along on an even keel; however, lack of balance leads to feelings of stress.

Stress causes problems with the brain's happy messengers. When life is smooth, happy messages keep up with demand. But when too much stress is placed on the brain, the happy messengers begin to fall behind on their deliveries.

As the stress continues, the happy messages begin to fail. Important nerve centres then receive mostly *sad messages*, and the whole brain becomes distressed. The person enters a state of brain chemical imbalance known as over-stress.

Over-stress makes people feel terrible. When sad messages overwhelm the happy messages, people can feel overwhelmed by life. They often complain of being tired, unable to fall asleep or maintain a restful night's sleep.

They have plagues of aches and pains, lack energy, and feel less enjoyment of life. Depression, anxiety, or just feeling unable to cope with life often ensues.

Find time for the things you enjoy and prioritise the things that are most important. Isolate all the key areas of your life and check to see if you have got the balance right.

Tip the balance back into your favour by making room for the happy messages! Some simple but effective ways include:

- Noticing something beautiful every day
- Daily appreciation of things you are grateful for
- Taking time to indulge and feed your passions
- Being with people who make you feel special
- Laughing
- Hanging out with children
- Keeping a daily log of at least one thing that makes you happy

Have you taken too much on? If so, what can you let go of? Remember to focus on one goal at a time; then it is achievable.

48

STEP AWAY

Workaholism is an addiction for many passionate people. Others use overwork to medicate their unhappiness in other areas of their life—most commonly dissatisfaction with their relationships.

When you work slavishly, particularly at something you love, your brain releases chemicals called opiates which create feelings of euphoria. No wonder it's hard to step away!

Euphoria stems from the Greek word *euphoría*—the power of enduring easily. But consider what the state of endurance implies. Enduring implies force or strain, or gritting your teeth and bearing it at times. Force or strain with no respite leads to stress, overload, and burnout—robbing you of vital energy and depleting your millionaire mindset.

Many people find when they don't step away from their work they suffer disillusionment, and things that once filled them with passion, including their current writing projects, no longer fills them with joy. Resentment builds and relationships with family, friends, and colleagues can also suffer.

Working addictively offers a short-term fix, but lasting happiness needs variety and nourishment. Being with family or friends, engaging in a hobby, spending time in nature, learning something new, helping others, or just being solitary will help you avoid burnout, nourish your brain, heart, and soul, improve your judgment, and restore harmony.

To be truly happy and successful, you must be able to be at peace when you are working and when you are at rest.

Leonardo da Vinci would often take breaks from his work to refresh his mind and spirit. While others claimed that he took too long to finish things, he knew the importance of replenishing his focus to maintain a clear perspective.

Here we are still talking about him over 500 years later.

"Every now and then go away, have a little relaxation, for when you come back to your work your judgment will be surer. Go some distance away because then the work appears smaller and more of it can be taken in at a glance and a lack of harmony and proportion is more readily seen," he once said.

Leonardo also valued sleep, noting in one of his journals that some of his best insights came when his mind was not working.

Even if you love the work that you do, and think your current obsession is the greatest thing since women were allowed to vote, it's fun to get away from it and have objective-free time to unwind and reset.

One of my author friends shared recently how she was feeling totally overwhelmed and close to burnout. To sustain her life, and her career, she's promising herself a reward for all her long hours—three-months off over winter. She's planning to go on a retreat, somewhere warm, maybe the Bahamas or Mexico.

"The whole point of living life is to enjoy it, right?! I'm coming to grips with that mindset," she wrote to me.

Schedule time out—and be firm with yourself. Stay away from anything that feeds your addiction.

When you return to your work, your focus will be surer, your vision refreshed, and your confidence bolder.

Rest

When your stress levels are high and you get depressed, angry, tense, and lethargic, or begin to experience tension headaches, it should be a very simple biofeedback signal that you need to stop, re-evaluate your choices and take some time out.

Sometimes this can be easier said than done. In our overachiever, overstimulated society, where many people spend more hours every week with their eyes riveted to their iPhone, instead of spending quality time on their own or with family and friends, the whole concept of stopping and resting to restore ourselves seems unusual. But resting to replenish is essential to well-being.

We're pushing ourselves all day long with energy that we don't have. The most common complaint people take to the doctor is fatigue. Research conducted by a company helping people suffering from adrenal fatigue claims that 80% of people don't have as much energy as they'd like to have.

"It's because we're pushing and using caffeine, sugar and energy drinks and nicotine and stress for energy rather than running on our own energy."

Long-term stress and long-term cortisol will literally alter a person's hormonal profile.

Rest allows the adrenal glands to restore, enabling cortisol levels to return to normal. Long-term stress and long-term cortisol overload can lead to adrenal fatigue and burn-out, altering your hormonal profile, changing your personality, and making it more difficult to return to the real, inspired, happy and creative you.

Give yourself permission to take time every day and every week to have fun, rest your mind and rest your body.

Get outside

It's hard to feel fantastic when you're suffering from low mood. Very often a lack of outside time is the culprit. You're like a flower—you need at least 20 minutes of sunlight every day just to make your hormones work effectively and enable you to blossom to your fullest potential.

To feel and behave normally you need to be exposed to full-spectrum daylight on a regular basis. Medical research suggests some people need as much as two hours a day of sunlight to avoid Seasonal Affective Disorder.

Combine outside time with exercise like walking and not only will you get the light you need, but you'll also recharge your batteries.

Walking outside can also help you gain a new perspective on a troubling situation. When you for a walk, you increase the electrical activity in your brain, and you breathe negative ions and see three-dimensionally.

All this helps you see with fresh eyes the things which are worrying you. Often you'll find that things are not as bad as they first appear, or discover a relatively simple solution.

Monitor how much time you spend indoors. Bounce away from habits that so many people have, like spending too many hours inside in front of two-dimensional computer monitors and TV screens, and then topping off a 12-hour day at work by trying to read themselves to sleep on their Kindle. These are all two-dimensional visual activities, which seldom spark joy.

Let mother earth, the sea, and the infinite sky boost your mood. Get outside and allow the sun and outside energy to lift your spirits. Schedule regular fresh air time. Improve your breathing, and take a brisk walk to increase your oxygen levels.

49

REST

When your stress levels are high and you get depressed, angry, tense, and lethargic or begin to experience tension headaches, etc., that should be a very simple biofeedback signal that you need to stop, re-evaluate your choices and take some time out.

Sometimes this can be easier said than done. In our overachiever, overstimulated society, where many people spend more hours every week with their eyes riveted to their iPhone, instead of spending quality time on their own or with family and friends, the whole concept of stopping and resting to restore ourselves seems unusual. But resting to replenish is essential to well-being.

We're pushing ourselves all day long with energy that we don't have. The most common complaint people take to the doctor for is fatigue. Research conducted by a company helping people suffering from adrenal fatigue claims that 80% of people don't have as much energy as they'd like to have.

"It's because we're pushing and using caffeine, sugar and energy drinks and nicotine and stress for energy rather than running on our own energy."

Long-term stress and long-term cortisol will literally alter a person's hormonal profile.

Rest allows the adrenal glands to restore, enabling cortisol levels to return to normal. Long-term stress and long-term cortisol overload can lead to adrenal fatigue and burn-out, altering your hormonal profile, and making it more difficult to return to the real, inspired, happy and creative you.

Give yourself permission to take time every day and every week to have fun, rest your mind and rest your body.

50

MASSAGE

One of my favourite ways to rest and exercise self-care is to go for a massage. But, so many people mistakenly think massage is an indulgence rather than a health-behaviour.

Some of the many benefits of massage include reduced stress and higher levels of neuroendocrine and immune functioning—which means better hormonal balance and more immunity to disease and illness.

Some studies also suggest that a one-hour massage results in benefits equivalent to a 6-hour sleep.

Sounds good to me, especially when I'm feeling fatigued.

If getting naked isn't your thing, consider an energy healing treatment with a trained Reiki practitioner.

Reiki is a Japanese word. **Rei** means *universal transcendental spirit* and **Ki** stands for *life energy*. Hence, the word carries a sense of universal life energy. Many scientific minds, as well as sage healers, have believed throughout the years that the universe is filled with this invisible life energy and that the life and health of all living beings are sustained by it.

Increasing evidence suggests that there does exist a superior *intelligent force* which contains all creation and out of which all life arises.

The energy of this force pervades all things and this is the energy that flows through our hands in concentrated form when we treat with Reiki.

Reiki healing is the ancient art of "hands-on healing" and offers a natural and holistic approach to mental, emotional, physical, and spiritual wellbeing.

You don't have to believe in any religion or be particularly spiritual to benefit from Reiki. It's an inclusive, non-religious form of healing and safe for everyone.

When I was experiencing a huge period of stress, I gained so much immediate benefit from my Reiki treatments that I decided to learn this beautiful healing technique. Recently in Bali, I completed my master level training.

You don't have to be Reiki-trained to live by the principles developed by Reiki founder Dr. Mikao Usui: "Just for today do not worry. Just for today do not anger. Honour your parents, teachers, and elders. Earn your living honestly. Show gratitude to everything."

Put more fuel in your tank and give yourself the gift of a therapeutic massage or Reiki treatment.

51

PRAYER THERAPY

Harness the energies of love and boost your ability to bounce and tenacity to succeed with the sacred daily ritual of prayer.

If prayer is something you are unfamiliar with or hold negative associations about, don't be deterred. Whatever your experience or belief system, prayer is simply a form of spiritual communion. It's a very simple and potent tool used successfully by many resilient people.

Many people have lost their union with God because of the hypocritical dogma which has polluted many faith systems. However, prayer comes in many shapes, colours, and textures.

Many prosperous creatives and successful business people, including Coco Chanel, Julia Cameron, Wayne Dyer, and Louise Hay, refer to prayer in several forms, including describing it as the voice of God, intuition, higher self, inner goddess, or their Sacred Divine.

In her book *Illuminata: A Return to Prayer*, Marianne Williamson speaks of prayer as a way of "focusing our eyes," dramatically transforming our orientation, releasing us "from the snares of lower energies," and aligning "our internal energies with truth."

As the author of *The Alchemist*, Paulo Coelho, shares on the back jacket of his book, *The Spy*, "In searching for his own place in the world, he has discovered answers for the challenges that everybody faces. He believes that within ourselves, we have the necessary strength to find our destiny."

Prayer, or invoking a higher power, is revered by many for its power to help them reclaim their strength, find their inner power and overcome tragedy.

In their book *The Energies of Love*, intuitive healer Donna Eden and psychiatrist David Feinstein refer to the action of prayer as inviting an inspiring invocation.

Dictionary.com refers to an invocation as the "act of invoking or calling upon a deity, spirit, etc., for aid, protection, inspiration, or the like." The website also defines invocation as "an entreaty for aid and guidance from a Muse."

Saying a simple prayer "alerts your sensibilities to dimensions that your senses do not perceive," say Eden and Feinstein.

In their book, they share how they are not consistent with their use of invocations, but use them most when they are about to embark on anything creative.

"Dozens of mini-prayers have infused the writing of this book, sometimes asking for wisdom, clarity, focus, and humour; other times asking that you, dear reader, receive guidance that gives your relationship greater ease, depth, healing, and joy."

Below are a few examples of their collective and individual invocations:

We ask that we touch people deeply and in ways that enhance their spirits, well-being, and mastery of their energies.

I ask this day for opportunities to love, to flourish, and to heal that which thirsts for healing.

I ask for support so that which is purest within me can shine through me.

Acting on the recommendation in their book to create my own invocation by referring to the writings of Rumi, one of my favourite poetic mystics, I wrote the below invocation from which I draw sustenance and purpose:

> I have one small drop of knowing in my soul. Fill my heart with wisdom and let it dissolve in your ocean (spreading healing waves of comfort, hope, and joy to all those who bathe in the waters of my creations.

Scientific (4-step) prayer therapy is another form of invoking guidance and "the only real answer to the great deception," writes Joseph Murphy (PhD.) in his excellent book, *The Miracle of Mind Dynamics*.

"Let the light of God shine in your mind, and you will neutralise the harmful effects of the negatives implanted in your subconscious mind."

The four steps Murphy suggests are:

• Recognition of the healing presence of Infinite Intelligence
• Complete acceptance of the One Power
• Affirmation of the Truth
• Rejoice and give thanks for the answer

"Faith is action in love," Mother Theresa once said. Whatever mode of prayer or invocation you use, read them slowly and deliberately and notice how the energies in your mind, body and soul shift.

The indicator of God's presence in you is the presence of peace, harmony, abundance, and joy.

Take the time to stop and pray from your heart. The words that you use aren't as important compared to the strength of your desire to connect with The Divine.

Be open to a response appearing which is different from your expectations—and know that your prayers are heard and answered.

52

CULTIVATE HOPE

Common obstacles to success include fear, self-doubt, and other crippling thoughts. But what if all you had to do to tame these uglies was cultivate hope?

The power of hope is grounded firmly in spiritual and religious practices but also in science. Like the ancient Greeks and Romans, Leonardo da Vinci, and even 18th-century physicians recognised the physiological effects of mind-power and hope on the body.

Successful medical outcomes, even when the intervention is a placebo, further evidence the impact of maintaining a positive expectation. If like me, you've manifested miracles in your own life, by maintaining a positive expectation, you'll know the power of hope.

Thoughts *do* become things. Scientists Gregg Braden and also Bruce Lipton, author of *The Biology of Belief*, have evidenced this.

But hope can only flourish when you believe that what you do can make a difference, that you recognise that you have choices and that your actions can create a future which differs from your present situation.

When you empower your belief in your ability to gain some control over your circumstances, you are no longer entirely at the mercy of forces outside yourself. You are back in the driving seat.

21 Ways to Turn Your Thoughts to Hope

1. Set achievement goals—not avoidance goals
2. Take steps—no matter how small, every day toward your goals
3. Create more joy
4. Surround yourself with positive, hopeful, optimistic people
5. Affirm the positive
6. Visualise a positive outcome
7. Pray
8. Journal your way to help
9. Be solution, not obstacle, focused
10. Let go. Hope has a harder job when you hang onto things that no longer serve you
11. Act as if
12. Manage your words, thoughts, and feelings
13. Tell yourself, "everything is working out for my highest good," or something similar when setbacks threaten to knock your hope
14. Remind yourself, "this too will pass," when crap happens. Nothing is permanent. Nothing!
15. Meditate
16. Colour therapy
17. Essential oils
18. Rest and sleep
19. Diet
20. Spirituality, faith
21. Let desire, not fear, lift you higher. Do the thing you fear and desire will triumph

"Fearlessness is like a muscle. I know from my own life that the more I exercise it the more natural it becomes to not let my fears run me," says businesswoman, author, and founder of *The Huffington Post*, Arianna Huffington.

What you believe has a tremendous influence on the likelihood of success. Reframe your fears and buoy your dreams with hope. Not "I'm afraid of failing," but "I hope to succeed," or something similar.

Would you rather be a failure at something you love than a failure at something you hate? It's a question worth considering.

How could you cultivate more hope? If you felt the fear and did it anyway, what's the best that could happen?

53

LAUGH AND PLAY

Laughter, humour, and play are great tonics during stressful times. Taking yourself or your life too seriously only increases stress. When you learn to laugh despite your difficulties, you light up the world.

"When people just look at your face," the Dalai Lama said to the Archbishop Desmond Tutu in *The Book of Joy*, "you are always laughing, always joyful. This is a very positive message. It is much better when there is not too much seriousness. Laughter, joking is much better. Then we can be completely relaxed."

Laughter triggers the release of endorphins, your brain's feel-good chemicals, setting off an emotional reaction which makes you feel better.

"Discovering more joy does not, I'm sorry to say, save us from the inevitability of hardship and heartbreak. In fact, we may cry more easily, but we will laugh more easily, too," says Archbishop Tutu.

"Perhaps we are just more alive. Yet as we discover more joy, we can face suffering in a way that ennobles rather than embitters. We have hardship without becoming hard. We have heartbreak without being broken."

You may not feel like it, but give laughter a go. Watch a funny movie, stream a stack of whacky comedies, go to a comedy show, or watch a video on YouTube. Hang out with people who know how to have a good time, go to a Laughing Yoga class, or ask someone to tickle you!

Inject some more laughter and playfulness into your life.

Playfulness is bounciness at its best. Cultivate your inner child. Act up a little, goof-off, experiment, relax and detach—if you find yourself in trouble, smile.

Benefits of play include:

- Increasing your productivity
- Boosting your creativity and problem-solving skills
- Reducing stress, anxiety, and depression
- Improving your relationships and connections with others
- Bringing more balance, fun, lightness, and levity into your life
- Diminishing your worries

As play researcher and psychiatrist Stuart Brown says in his book *Play: How it Shapes the Brain, Opens the Imagination, and Invigorates the Soul*, "A lack of play should be treated like malnutrition: it's a health risk to your body and mind."

The Dalai Lama agrees. "I met some scientists in Japan, and they explained that wholehearted laughter—not artificial laughter—is very good for your heart and your health in general."

Some of the many ways I play include: 'wagging' work sometimes and taking my inner child on a playdate to the movies, going for a massage, or indulging in my hobbies and playing with my paints.

Listening to music from the 70s is also playful and brings levity. While traveling internationally recently, I watched the Disney children's movie *Frozen*. I haven't laughed so much in years.

I also love reminding myself of the magic of writing and reading. As novelist Caroline Gordon once wrote, "A well-composed book is a magic carpet on which we are wafted to a world that we cannot enter in any other way."

Author Deepak Chopra confirms the power of lightening up,

"When we harness the forces of harmony, joy, and love, we create success and good fortune with effortless ease," Chopra says.

Check out my blog for some strategies to reinforce play and create more bounciness in your day—https://www.cassandragaisford.com/how-to-stress-less-and-play-more/

54

SMELL YOUR WAY TO HAPPINESS

Along with your skills and capabilities, it is your state of mind that determines how happy you will be.

There are many ways to empower your mind—working with essential oils is one of the most effortless. The sense of smell is the most basic and primitive of all our senses and is of vital importance to your well-being.

The process of smelling is called olfaction and is incredibly complicated, taking place in several areas of the brain including the limbic system which itself has approximately 34 structures and 53 pathways. The limbic system is linked to sensations of pleasure and pain, and emotions— both positive and negative, including fear and confidence, sadness and joy and other feelings that can either erode or boost productivity and prosperity.

The simple truth is that even if you are unaware of the power of smell, aroma affects your mood.

Scientists now believe that all our emotions are the result of neurochemicals such as noradrenaline and serotonin being released into the bloodstream. Mood swings are thought to be a result of these influences, particularly when they are in the extreme.

Given these facts, it's not hard to see how essential oils can help balance and influence our thoughts, feelings, and behaviours.

"Feeling educated about essential oils is such an empowering experience because there are so many different oils you can work with," writes Clinical Aromatherapist Andrea Butje in her book, *The Heart of Aromatherapy: An Easy-to-Use Guide for Essential Oils.*

"They all offer the nourishment of the plant they are distilled from in a single drop, and education helps you understand which oils to reach for at which times. Nature works holistically...and so do we."

As I share in my book, *The Art of Success: How Extraordinary Artists Can Help You Succeed in Business and Life,* Coco Chanel knew the alchemical potency of flowers and plants. She surrounded herself with nature's elixir and amassed a fortune from the essential oils which helped make her perfume Chanel N°5 famous.

The transcendent alchemy of the potions that went into the Chanel N°5 formula was not left to chance. Grieving after her lover Boy Chapel's death, Coco drew upon the essences of jasmine, ylang-ylang, vetiver, and other restorative scents to imbue Coco's Chanel N°5 with hope, healing, and the sensual confidence that love lost would be found again.

Aromatherapy, using the scents of plants and flowers, is one of many ancient remedies validated by modern science today. It's the Swiss army knife of all things healing—physically, mentally, spiritually, and emotionally.

There are so many different essential oils that can help you. Here are a few essential oils and natural therapeutic remedies to help increase your alertness and refresh and uplift your mind, body, and spirit:

• Laurel Essential Oil: Motivates people who lack energy or confidence. It also strengthens the memory and helps maintain concentration, especially during prolonged tasks

• Rosemary Essential Oil: Instills confidence during periods of self-doubt and keeps motivation levels high when the going gets tough. It is also said to help maintain an open mind and to make you more accepting of new ideas.

• Cardamom Essential Oil: Stimulates a dull mind, dispels tensions and worries, and nurtures and supports the brain and nervous system. Many people find it of great support during challenging times.

• Peppermint Essential Oil: With its refreshing scent peppermint works as a power boost for your fatigued mind, making you feel sharper and more alert.

ALERTNESS:
- Ginger 6 drops
- Grapefruit 5 drops
- Juniper Berry 4 drops
- 15 ml of a carrier oil

ENERGISING:
- Lavender 8 drops
- Lemon 2 drops
- Orange 6 drops
- Rosemary 4 drops

Aromatherapy for emotional well-being

The use of essential oils for emotional well-being is what is first thought of when someone thinks of the term "aromatherapy."

Although aromatherapy should not be considered a miracle cure for more serious emotional issues, the use of essential oils can assist, some-times greatly, with certain emotional issues.

For example, lavender is a well-known mild analgesic, useful for healing headaches, wounds, calming the nerves, insomnia, and mild depression.

Rosemary, on the other hand, is a mild stimulant and is used to treat physical and mental fatigue, forgetfulness, and respiratory problems among other ailments.

Stress-Relieving Blends

These blends stated below can help during times of stress. When selecting and using oils, be sure to follow all safety precautions and remember that aromatherapy should not be used as a substitute for proper medical treatment.

Blend 1
• Three drops Clary Sage, one drop Lemon, one drop Lavender
Blend 2
• Two drops Romance Chamomile, two drops Lavender, one drop Vetiver
Blend 3
• Three drops Bergamot, one drop Geranium, one drop Frankincense
Blend 4
• Three drops Grapefruit, one drop Jasmine, one drop Ylang Ylang

Directions:
1. Select one of the blends shown above.
2. Choose how you'd like to use the blend and follow the directions below:

Diffuser Blend

Multiply your blend by four to obtain a total of 20 drops of your chosen blend. Add your oils to a dark coloured glass bottle and mix well by rolling the bottle in between your hands. Add the appropriate number of drops from your created blend to your diffuser by following the manufacturer's instructions.

Bath Oil

Multiply your blend by three to obtain a total of 15 drops of your chosen blend.

. . .

BATH SALTS

Continue by using the five drops, blend with Bath Salts.

MASSAGE OIL

Multiply your blend by two to obtain a total of 10 drops of your chosen blend.

AIR FRESHENER

Multiply your blend by six to obtain a total of 30 drops of your chosen blend.

Investigate the power of aromatherapy. What scents imbue you with confidence? Courage? Productivity? Sharpen your most potent tools—your heart and your mind. Become a perfumer—experiment with essential oils until you find a winning blend.

Create your own success blend, or have an expert create one for you. Beginning with how you want to feel is a good place to start.

55
BOUNCE WITH COLOUR

Colour has a profound effect on us at all levels - physical, mental, emotional, and spiritual.

We are in a world where colour dominates our lives, from reading signs on the road to identifying ripe fruit by its colour.

Colour affects our moods. Blue is calming. Red can make us tense. We use colour every day in our lives without even appreciating it.

Decide on the mood you want to be in and choose a colour that makes you feel that way. For example, if you want to feel calm, you may choose green or blue.

Remember that colour is individually perceived, so choose what works for you. On some days red may make you feel energised, on others it may fuel feelings of anger or aggression.

You may want to wear your bouncy colour in your clothes, or just to have a small dose of colour nearby to prompt these feelings along – for example, it may be some colour on your desktop or on a prompt card by your PC or in your wallet.

Wearing colour also sparks joy in others. As a shop assistant recently said to me, "You have just made my day with how pink and sparkly you are."

The right colour can also empower you and give you the courage and strength of a warrior. During a particularly stressful time in my life, and that of my daughter's, I had to rescue her from the clutches of a former patched gang member. It was also like a scene in a movie. I wore white. White lace, in fact. Elegant, chic, peaceful—and regal. He wore black. Dark. Low. Fierce.

Before I arrived to meet him, I visualised white light all around me. I prayed for help from my angels and guides, and importantly I sent love to this wounded, but dangerous man. Love and the white light won. He surrendered my daughter back to me—something this dominating, controlling man had previously refused to do.

What colours feed your courage? What hues boost your resilience? Surround yourself with colours that empower you and spark joy and banish those that don't.

56

BOUNCE YOUR KNOWLEDGE

Knowledge is power. No matter what your situation, no matter what your current level of expertise or knowledge, always, always be informed. Not everybody has your best interests in mind, and everyone is capable of mistakes.

When you empower your mind with the knowledge you need you'll feel more in control and boost your capacity to bounce.

When I was building my home all the experts told me everything was fine. But I had heard of planned changes to the building code and became alarmed. In short, I had to battle with my architect, with the local council, and with my builders in my quest to have them make the required changes to the design.

At the time of gathering all the knowledge I needed, I didn't feel like I was bouncing at all. I felt incredibly frustrated and over-whelmed. But then, when I went to sell my home and the new owners found that the house met the new building code require-ments, I felt a spring in my step. My house sold easily.

Other homeowners weren't so lucky, and have been stuck with sub-standard homes they can't sell and have had to try and recover damages from their architects, builders, and councils.

Similarly, when an intruder tried to break into my rural property the police told me not to worry. But the man kept coming back. The police said he was harmless. I told them harmless men don't threaten me or my partner with violence.

I had to become informed about how to have a trespass notice issued correctly—the police kept giving me conflicting advice. Finally, I said, "I will not be the woman people read about in the paper—the one who was assaulted by an intruder and was murdered."

In the process of finding out the right way to deter an intruder, I reclaimed my safety, my peace of mind and my power.

Many of my clients who have been experiencing bullying at work have done the same. They have found out their legal rights, either for themselves or with the help of an employment lawyer, and have taken back their power.

Sometimes, this has been by learning to be more assertive, or by realising their job sucked and finding another one, or working for themselves.

Similarly, my partner queried the medical advice his doctor gave him recently. Often doctors are too quick to prescribe medication without having first completed a full diagnosis—including asking about lifestyle factors that may be contributing to poor health.

My partner had done considerable research into the side effects of the medication he was given for his blood pressure, and was alarmed that his doctor's response to his concerns was to prescribe more medication to reduce the side effects of the first medication.

Google 'scary side effects of medication' and you may be alarmed. But a cautionary note, don't stop taking any medication without checking your facts—you may risk worsening your original condition.

Whatever your situation, bounce your knowledge—become informed.

57

ALWAYS BOUNCE BACK

Resilient people are flexible, they bend with the winter gales and arc with the summer breeze. When the fury of a hurricane knocks them down, they get back up again—and it's the getting back up that elevates your bounce.

When you get back up life will reward you for your efforts. It may not be instant, it may not happen the very same day, but it will happen. That's what you must keep believing in.

What is certain is that unless you put in the energy nothing good will happen at all.

Taking empowered action may result in better health, improved relationships, improved finances, and respect and admiration from people for your courage, tenacity, and perseverance.

"You're like a cat with nine lives," a friend once said to me, following a particularly traumatic breakup. "You always land on your feet."

I've been a single mother, receiving no financial support from my daughter's father. I survived a very challenging childhood. I've experienced the most horrific workplace bullying. I've been physically assaulted, intimidated and threatened. And I've also had to rescue my daughter from the fists of a violent man.

I've had to face my fears of public speaking, criticism, failure and standing out. I've had to empower my mind, body, and spirit with new tools—many of which I have shared in this book. Meditation, mind power, spiritual-based practices, nutrition, counselling, reading self-empowerment books, like this one—and more.

I've worked hard to cultivate courage, optimism, and resilience. In fact, one lady I worked with once said, "You know what your problem is Cassandra? You're too happy."

I knew the bigger problem, the one that lurked inside, was a tendency to be too sad. I decided what I wanted more of.

Happiness.

Feeling sad, staying down,—well, it just doesn't spark joy.

I know what it's like to feel so low that you don't think you can go on. I know what it's like to contemplate ending your life. I know a great many people feel the same. And it's these people, the ones with the will to survive who work every day, as the Dalai Lama urges, to cultivate happiness, optimism, a resilient mindset—and to pay it forward by helping others.

As Robbie Williams once sang, "I get knocked down, but I get back up again. You're never gonna keep me down."

And you can, and will too.

58

PASSION JOURNAL TIPS

It's staggeringly, and dishearteningly, true that many people don't know what they are passionate about. Some research suggests that only 10% of people are living and working with passion.

Hence my passion for passion— to bring about positive change in the world. Creating a passion journal is one simple but powerful technique to help achieve this.

The purpose of the Passion Journal is to encourage you to create and stay focused on your preferred future and goals and to build greater awareness of your own unique passion criteria.

The Passion Journal taps into the principles of The Law of Attraction and Law of Intention to help you manifest your dreams.

It acts as a central, easily retrievable place to collect and store sources of inspiration, insights, and clues related to your passion, career goals, and preferred future. It is also a motivational tool to be updated regularly and looked at frequently—ideally daily.

According to mind-mapping and creativity expert Tony Buzan, we think in images, not words. Surround yourself with images that symbolise or reflect the things you want to create. Allow these images to inspire and excite you. Add a dose of colour and engage all your senses.

Keeping a journal gives you a sense of your own story. In a sense, you create a script for your own life as you go along.

I was clearing out some of my old journals the other day when I came across something I had written back in 2000. "I will live in a house that is elevated with lots of sunshine, and which is surrounded by trees. It will be elegant and streamlined, with simplicity at its core and feng-shuied to make sure it is the best it can be."

What amazed me was not what I had written but the astonishing realisation that seven years later I was living in the house I had created first in my imagination.

I achieved the same result when I began manifesting moving to a lifestyle property. I now live on a gorgeous 10-acre property overlooking the beautiful Bay of Islands.

I have done the same thing in my career. Gathering images of the ingredients of career satisfaction, helped me see my way to career success and to direct my job creation activities much more efficiently.

I even manifested my dream man! Now, that's powerful creativity!

It's also one of the principals of the Law of Attraction made infamous by the DVD *The Secret*. But guess what? There is no secret! What there is instead is a lack of conscious awareness about how to tap into the law of attraction to make your dreams and goals a reality.

Creating your Passion Journal

Choosing the right book and designing your cover

To be effective choose a journal no smaller than A4 with blank pages—to free up your linear brain it's important there are no lines.

The cover of your journal is very important. Every time you look at it, it will reinforce your key theme/s. Choose a colour or image for the front cover which symbolises what you want to experience, or how you want to feel about your future. These colours and images will reinforce optimism and purpose on a subconscious level and help you maintain your focus.

If you can't find a journal with the ideal cover don't let this stop you. Create one. Every year I go to my local art store and choose a blank A4 visual diary with a hard white cover. I then create my theme.

One year I drew a simple red circle – symbolising (for me) spirituality, the Divine Feminine, going with the flow and many other themes important to me that year.

In 2014, I created the cover of my passion journal by gluing a photo of a painting I purchased by one of my favourite artists, Max Gimblett, who is also a Zen Buddhist monk.

I included a quote, and added the words: "The art spirit." This reinforced my key theme of focusing on my creativity that year. The colour of the painting was important to me, too, violet and green, symbolising spirituality, growth, and renewal.

Other clients have chosen a single image or a colour such as yellow (to boost optimism). Again, there is no right way— only the way that speaks to who you are and who you choose to be.

Unleash your creativity

Adding lots of images and colour is an important part of manifesting your desires. Gather anything that matches or provides clues to your passion.

These may be clippings from magazines, words and phrases that affirm what you want, pictures of people who are doing the sort of work you want to do, or who inspire you in any way.

Add any other inspirational information and imagery that affirms and reinforces your intentions. Get your felt tip pens out, a glue stick and scissors and unchain your inner child.

You may also want to paste logos of companies you want to work for—or create your own logo if you dream of self-employment.

Add job advertisements and position descriptions that excite you.

If more romance is what you're after, or better health and worklife balance—you know what to do!

59

SUMMARY OF HOLISTIC BOUNCE STRATEGIES

Throughout this book, you've discovered ways to overcome adversity, build resilience and find joy by increasing your ability to cope. Regular exercise, a good diet, relaxation exercises, and rest are a few of the many techniques we've covered.

You've also discovered ways to feed your soul and achieve your highest potential—following your passion, jumping with joy and bouncing high...and more.

Listed below are some helpful reminders of some of the many holistic coping strategies you can call upon during times of current or anticipated need.

Physical

- Learn to listen to your body
- Adequate exercise
- Physical touch/massage
- Muscle relaxation
- Sleep
- Warmth

- Relaxation breathing
- A healthy diet, i.e. reducing stimulants (coffee, nicotine, etc.), increasing water, and eating organic non-processed foods
- Yoga

Behavioral

- Balanced lifestyle
- Support groups / Counselling
- Sharing with friends and family
- Humour
- New interests / activities
- Hobbies
- Socialising
- Entertaining
- Taking time out
- Music / dancing / singing/creative expression
- Meditating
- Yoga
- Being proactive and taking control of the situation
- Change careers
- Reducing or eliminating alcohol consumption
- Making time to do nothing at all

Cognitive / Perceptual (thinking)

- Rational thinking techniques to help change the way you interpret the stressful situation
- Positive thinking/cultivating optimism
- Self-assertion training
- Personal development
- Building self-esteem
- Realistic goal planning

- Time management
- Learning to say "No"
- Priority clarification
- Reflection
- Mindfulness
- Acceptance
- Hypnosis

Emotional

- Releasing emotions and expressing feelings (laugh, talk, cry, write in a journal, paint, etc.)
- Learning how to "switch off"
- Taking time out
- Solitude and space
- Intimacy
- Counselling and support
- Challenging your emotional reactions to situations
- Passion/Joy

Social

- Scheduling time to spend with important people in your life
- Making plans with friends, family and loved ones in advance
- Sharing your experiences of stress with certain people in your life, especially letting them know the ways that stress has been affecting you, so they understand
- Practicing assertive communication within your significant relationships to decrease conflicts, while also continuing to find ways to show people around you that they are important

Spiritual

• Prayer and mediation—scheduling regular time
• Helping others (talking, writing, supporting)
• Reiki and other energy healing techniques
• Talking with a spiritual confidant or leader to explain any spiritual issues or doubts that you may have encountered
• Forgiveness (of self or others)
• Compassion / loving kindness
• Continuing to read and learn about your faith, belief or value system
• Connecting with others who share your beliefs

60

YOUR CREATING BOUNCE AND BUILDING RESILIENCE PLAN

Reflect back on the strategies and tools you've discovered in this book. Complete the following exercise to create your personal action plan for managing stress and building resilience:

Personal Action Plan for Creating Bounce and Building Resilience

- Factors in your work and life that are causing you the greatest stress are:

- The four coping strategies which you know work for you in dealing with stress are:

- Your no-excuses strategy to make a commitment to put one or more of these strategies into practice at least once a day is:.

- The positive phrase you will use to help change your level of stress is:

- Put this phrase where you can see it and say it to yourself when you start to feel stressed.

COMPLETE THE FOLLOWING:

I SHALL STOP DOING:

I SHALL DO LESS:

I SHALL DO MORE:

I SHALL START TO DO:

CONCLUSION

I hope this book has helped you to focus on your best life—regardless of any unfavourable or challenging outer conditions imposed on you by the physical world.

Thoughts really do become things and you will reap what you plant in your field of dreams.

Adopt a bouncy mindset—dream big, be audacious, take inspired action, and fear less. Live more and experience the extraordinary life that awaits you. The power to live a significant life lies within you.

Bouncing through life can mean counting your blessings for even the simplest, and often the most valuable, things and may include:

- Enjoying good health and mobility
- Being loved and loving in return
- Tapping into your infinite potential
- The ability to say, think, do, and write what you truly feel
- Living in a beautiful part of the world
- The ability to enchant and inspire others with your words
- Healing the world
- Inspiring others with your courage
- Feeling happy with yourself

- Fulfilment
- Living authentically
- Being audacious
. . . Or something else.

What matters most is not how you overcome obstacles to success. What matters is how meaningful the end result is for you.

Take care of yourself and your heart, and nourish your beautiful brain. All will follow. This is practical, this is inspired, this is how life works.

If you continue to exercise self-care and bounce with joy and child-like curiosity through life, and adopt a spirit of playfulness through challenging times, then this unknown and unpredictable life will manifest in favourable outcomes—for you, for those you love, and those drawn to you because of the beauty, power, and magic of who you are.

You may think the outcome has to happen in a certain way, on a certain day, but you can't always predict how life will bounce. Human willpower cannot make everything happen. Spirit has its own idea, of how the arrow flies, and upon which wind it travels.

It may not happen overnight, but if you follow your heart, maintain your focus, and take inspired action, your time will come.

I promise!

If by some strange twist of fate, it doesn't, at least you'll know you tried. A life of no regrets—now that's worth striving for.

Let the beauty you love be the life that you live.

Now go forth and bounce!

To your happiness and joy, and with love,

Cassandra

P.S. I truly hoped you enjoyed *Bounce*. I'm excited about the possibilities to take this simple but profound message of resilience and joy out into the world. Everyone needs encouragement and help to keep bouncing through life—especially those most vulnerable.

My next book is devoted to helping young people to bounce through setbacks, uncertainty and to inspire hope that they too, regardless of their upbringing can live joyfully.

Sign up for my newsletter to be the first to know when new books are released, and receive practical tips to bounce bountifully here >>

Be the first to know when my guided meditations and self-hypnosis audios are released, and stay tuned for news of my online courses, webinars and international retreats in exotic, empowering locations.

Sign up here http://eepurl.com/bEArfT

ALSO BY CASSANDRA GAISFORD

Transformational Super Kids:

The Little Princess
The Little Princess Can Fly
I Have to Grow
The Boy Who Cried
Jojo Lost Her Confidence

Mid-Life Career Rescue:

The Call for Change
What Makes You Happy
Employ Yourself
Job Search Strategies That Work
3 Book Box Set: The Call for Change, What Makes You Happy, Employ Yourself
4 Book Box Set: The Call for Change, What Makes You Happy, Employ Yourself, Job Search Strategies That Work

Career Change:

Career Change 2020 5 Book-Bundle Box Set

Master Life Coach:

Leonardo da Vinci: Life Coach
Coco Chanel: Life Coach

The Art of Living:

How to Find Your Passion and Purpose
How to Find Your Passion and Purpose Companion Workbook
Career Rescue: The Art and Science of Reinventing Your Career and Life
Boost Your Self-Esteem and Confidence
Anxiety Rescue
No! Why 'No' is the New 'Yes'
How to Find Your Joy and Purpose
How to Find Your Joy and Purpose Companion Workbook

The Art of Success:

Leonardo da Vinci
Coco Chanel

Journaling Prompts Series:

The Passion Journal
The Passion-Driven Business Planning Journal
How to Find Your Passion and Purpose 2 Book-Bundle Box Set

Health & Happiness:

The Happy, Healthy Artist
Stress Less. Love Life More
Bounce: Overcoming Adversity, Building Resilience and Finding Joy
Bounce Companion Workbook

Mindful Sobriety:

Mind Your Drink: The Surprising Joy of Sobriety
Mind Over Mojitos: How Moderating Your Drinking Can Change Your Life:
Easy Recipes for Happier Hours & a Joy-Filled Life
Your Beautiful Brain: Control Alcohol and Love Life More

Happy Sobriety:

Happy Sobriety: Non-Alcoholic Guilt-Free Drinks You'll Love
The Sobriety Journal
*Happy Sobriety Two Book Bundle-Box Set: Alcohol and Guilt-Free Drinks
You'll Love* & *The Sobriety Journal*

Money Manifestation:

*Financial Rescue: The Total Money Makeover: Create Wealth, Reduce Debt
& Gain Freedom*

The Prosperous Author:

Developing a Millionaire Mindset
Productivity Hacks: Do Less & Make More
Two Book Bundle-Box Set (Books 1-2)

Miracle Mindset:

*Change Your Mindset: Millionaire Mindset Makeover: The Power of
Purpose, Passion, & Perseverance*

Non-Fiction:

Where is Salvator Mundi?

More of Cassandra's practical and inspiring workbooks on a range of career and life-enhancing topics are on her website (www.cassandragaisford.com) and her author page at all good online bookstores.

NOW IN AUDIO!

Did you know you can enjoy and be inspired by Cassandra's most popular and successful books on audio? In less than 15 minutes you could be listening your way to a new life!

Check out the following written and narrated by Cassandra:

Mid-Life Career Rescue: The Career For Change
How to Find Your Passion and Purpose
The Little Princess
I Have to Grow
The Boy Who Cried

Audio versions of these and other titles available now from all online bookstores and libraries.

FOLLOW YOUR PASSION TO PROSPERITY ONLINE COURSE

If you need more help to find and live your life purpose you may prefer to take my online course, and watch inspirational and practical videos and other strategies to help you fulfill your potential.

Follow your passion and purpose to prosperity—online coaching program

Easily discover your passion and purpose, overcoming barriers to success, and create a job or business you love with my self-paced online course.

Gain unlimited lifetime access to this course, for as long as you like—across any and all devices you own. Be supported with practical, inspirational, easy-to-access strategies to achieve your dreams.

To start achieving outstanding personal and professional results with absolute certainty and excitement. **Click here to enroll or find out more— https://the-coaching-lab.teachable.com/p/follow-your-passion-and-purpose-to-prosperity**

FURTHER RESOURCES

Surf The Net

Mathew Johnstone has a wide range of books and resources on mental wellness and mindfulness: www.matthewjohnstone.com.au

www.whatthebleep.com—a powerful and inspiring site emphasizing quantum physics and the transformational power of thought.

www.heartmath.org—comprehensive information and tools help you access your intuitive insight and heart-based knowledge. Validated and supported by science-based research. Check out the additional information about your heart-brain.

Join polymath Tim Ferris and learn from his interesting and informative guests on The Tim Ferris Show http:// fourhourworkweek.com/podcast/.

Listen to podcasts which inspire you to become the best version of your writing self—*Joanna Penn's podcast* is very helpful for "authorpreneurs" http://www.thecreativepenn.com/podcasts. I also love Neil

Patel's   podcast   for   savvy   marketing   strategies
http://neilpatel.com/podcast.

Experience the transformative power of hypnosis. One of my favorite
hypnosis sites is the UK-based Uncommon Knowledge. On their
website http://www.hypnosisdownloads.com you'll find a range of
self-hypnosis mp3 audios, including The Millionaire Mindset
program.

Celebrity hypnotherapist and author Marissa Peer is another
favorite source of subconscious reprogramming and liberation
—www.marisapeer.com.

What beliefs are holding you back? Check out Peer's Youtube clip
"How To Teach Your Mind That Everything Is Available To You" here
—https://www.youtube.com/watch?v=IKeaAbM2kJg

Enjoy James Clear's fabulous blog content and receive further
self-improvement tips based on proven scientific research: http://
jamesclear.com/articles

Tim Ferriss recommends a couple of apps for those wanting some
help getting started with meditation—Headspace (www.
headspace.com) or Calm (www.calm.com).

National Geographic: The Science of Stress: Portrait of a killer
https://www.youtube.com/watch?v=ZyBsy5SQxqU

Effects of Stress on Your Body
https://www.youtube.com/watch?v=1p6EeYwp1O4

Mindfulness training
Wellington-based Peter Fernando offers an introductory guided
meditation which you can take further. He also meets with individ-
uals and groups in Wellington for philosophical talks on mindfulness
and Buddhism. Very enjoyable and great for the soul.
http://www.monthofmindfulness.info

Guided meditations
    www.calm.com

Free app with guided meditations
    http://eocinstitute.org/meditation/emotional-benefits-of-meditation/
    Includes a comprehensive list of the benefits of meditation.

Career Guidance Sites:
    www.aarp.org/work - information and tools to help you stay current and connected with what's hot and what's not in today's workplace.

www.lifereimagined.org - loads of inspiration and practical tips to help you maximize your interests and expertise, personalized and interactive.

www.whatthebleep.com – a powerful and inspiring site emphasizing quantum physics and the transformational power of thought.

www.personalitytype.com—created by the authors of *Do What You Are: Discover the Perfect Career for You through the Secrets of Personality Type*. This site focuses on expanding your awareness of your own type and that of others—including children and partners. This site also contains many useful links.

Books

Master your millionaire mindset with T. Harv Eker's book, *Secrets of the Millionaire Mind: Mastering the Inner Game of Wealth*.

Find your ONE thing with Gary Keller in *The One Thing: The Surprisingly Simple Truth Behind Extraordinary Results*.

Learn from masters in a diverse cross-section of fields—pick up a copy of Tim Ferriss' *Tool of Titans*.

Celebrate being an outlier and learn why clocking up 10,000

hours will help you succeed in Malcolm Gladwell's *Outliers: The Story of Success*.

Struggling in an extroverted world? Introverts are enjoying a renaissance, fueled in part by Susan Cain's terrific bestseller, *Quiet: The Power of Introverts in a World That Can't Stop Talking*.

Copy-cat your way to success with Austin Kleon's great book, *Steal Like An Artist*.

Roll up your sleeves and bring out the big guns to win your creative battle with *The War of Art* by Steven Pressfield.

Power up with a new personality—read Breaking the Habit of Being Yourself: How to Lose Your Mind and Create a New One by Dr. Joe Dispenza.

Unleash the power of your mind by reading *You Are the Placebo: Making Your Mind Matter,* by Dr. Joe Dispenza.

Manifest your prosperity with Rhonda Byrne in her popular book, *The Secret*.

Ensure you don't starve by reading Jeff Goins collated wisdom in *Real Artists Don't Starve: Timeless Strategies for Thriving in the New Creative Age*.

Fortify your faith with Julia Cameron's book, *Faith and Will*.

How to Survive and Thrive in Any Life Crisis, Dr. Al Siebert

Thrive: The Third Metric to Redefining Success and Creating a Happier Life, Arianna Huffington

(This book has great content throughout and some excellent resources listed in the back.)

The Power of Now: A Guide to Spiritual Enlightenment, Eckhart Tolle

The Book of Joy, The Dalai Lama and Archbishop Desmond Tutu

The Sleep Revolution: Transforming Your Life One Night at a Time, Arianna Huffington

Quiet the Mind: An Illustrated Guide on How to Meditate, Mathew Johnstone

Comfortable with Uncertainty: 108 Teachings on Cultivating Fearlessness and Compassion, Pema Chodron

Power vs. Force: The Hidden Determinants of Human Behavior, David R. Hawkins

Learn how to live an inspired life with Tarot cards and other oracles. Read Jessa Crispin's book, *The Creative Tarot: A Modern Guide to an Inspired Life.*

Check out all of Collette-Baron-Reid's books, including: *Uncharted: The Journey Through Uncertainty to Infinite Possibility* and *Messages from Spirit: The Extraordinary Power of Oracles, Omens, and Signs.*

PLEASE LEAVE A REVIEW

Word of mouth is the most powerful marketing force in the universe. If you found this book useful, I'd appreciate you rating this book and leaving a review. You don't have to say much—just a few words about how the book helped you learn something new or made you feel.

"Your books are a fantastic resource and until now I never even thought to write a review. Going forward I will be reviewing more books. So many great ones out there and I want to support the amazing people that write them."
Great reviews help people find good books.

Thank you so much! I appreciate you!

PS: If you enjoyed this book, do me a small favor to help spread the word about it and share on Facebook, Twitter and other social networks.

BLOSSOM

"Blossom into your dharma, that which you are meant to become. It is the music you are playing out in the world."
~ Pam Gregory

ABOUT THE AUTHOR

Cassandra Gaisford, is a holistic therapist, award-winning artist, and #1 bestselling author. A corporate escapee, she now lives and works from her idyllic lifestyle property overlooking the Bay of Islands in New Zealand.

Cassandra is best known for the passionate call to redefine what it means to be successful in today's world.

She is a well-known expert in the area of success, passion, purpose and transformational business, career and life change, and is regularly sought after as a keynote speaker, and by media seeking an expert opinion on career and personal development issues.

Cassandra has also contributed to international publications and been interviewed on national radio and television in New Zealand and America.

She has a proven-track record of success helping people find savvy ways to boost their finances, change careers, build a business or become a solopreneur—on a shoestring.

Cassandra's unique blend of business experience and qualifications (BCA, Dip Psych.), creative skills, and well-ness and holistic training (Dip Counselling, Reiki Master Teacher) blends pragmatism and commercial savvy with rare and unique insight and out-of-the-box-thinking for anyone wanting to achieve an extraordinary life.

STAY IN TOUCH

Become a fan and Continue To Be Supported, Encouraged, and Inspired

Subscribe to my newsletter and follow me on BookBub (https://www.bookbub.com/profile/cassandra-gaisford) and be the first to know about my new releases and giveaways

www.cassandragaisford.com
www.facebook.com/cassandra.gaisford
www.instagram.com/cassandragaisford
www.youtube.com/cassandragaisfordnz
www.pinterest.com/cassandraNZ
www.linkedin.com/in/cassandragaisford
www.twitter.com/cassandraNZ

And please, do check out some of my videos where I share strategies and tips to stress less and love life more—http://www.youtube.com/cassandragaisfordnz

BLOG

Subscribe and be inspired by regular posts to help you increase your wellness, follow your bliss, slay self-doubt, and sustain healthy habits.

Learn more about how to achieve happiness and success at work and life by visiting my blog:

www.cassandragaisford.com/archives

SPEAKING EVENTS

Cassandra is available internationally for speaking events aimed at wellness strategies, motivation, inspiration and as a keynote speaker.

She has an enthusiastic, humorous and passionate style of delivery and is celebrated for her ability to motivate, inspire and enlighten.

For information navigate to www.cassandragaisford.com/contact/speaking

To ask Cassandra to come and speak at your workplace or conference, contact: cassandra@cassandragaisford.com

NEWSLETTERS

For inspiring tools and helpful tips subscribe to Cassandra's free newsletters here:
http://www.cassandragaisford.com

Sign up now and receive a free eBook to help you find your passion and purpose!
http://eepurl.com/bEArfT

ACKNOWLEDGMENTS

This book (and my new life) was made possible by the amazing generosity, open-heartedness, and wonderful friendship of so many people. Thank you!

Sir Edmund Hillary often said that even Mount Everest wasn't climbed alone. A great achievement, or in my case a good book, is a product of collaboration. This project has, at times, loomed larger than the highest mountain in the world. I could not have persevered without the tremendous encouragement from a wealth of supportive and talented people.

To all the amazingly interesting clients who have allowed me to help them over the years, and to the wonderful people who read my newspaper columns and wrote to me with their stories of reinvention —thank you. Your feedback, deep sharing, requests for help, and inspired, courageous action continues to inspire me.

I'd also like to say a special thanks to the staff at *The Dominion Post* newspaper who gave me my first break into published writing. This book would never have existed had they not acted on my suggestion that a careers column would be a great idea. For over four years they gave me the encouragement and artistic freedom to write freely on a range of topics—all with the goal of helping to encourage and inspire others.

I'm also grateful to the Health Editor of *Marie Claire* magazine whom, after she had accepted a short article, said I had the bones of a good book and should write it.

A huge thank you also to my amazing Bounce Buddies, including Cate Walker, once again, for your beautiful and thorough editing. Thank you also to the advance readers who provided additional feedback and suggested improvements—Tina Drummond, Sheree Clark, Catherine Sloan, Heather Dodge, and many others, I am truly blessed to have received your input and cheerleading.

My thanks also to my terrific friends and supporters. And, of course, I can never say thank you enough to my family, particularly my parents and grandparents, who have instilled me with such tremendous values and life skills.

My daughter, Hannah—I wish for you everything that your heart desires. Without you, I doubt I would ever have accomplished all the things I have in my life.

Thank you.

FREE WORKBOOK!

The Passion Journal: The Effortless Path to Manifesting Your Love, Life, and Career Goals

Thank you for your interest in my new book.
To show my appreciation, I'm excited to be giving you another book for FREE!

Download the free *Passion Journal Workbook* here>>https://dl. bookfunnel.com/aepj97k2n1

I hope you enjoy it—it's dedicated to helping you live and work with passion, resilience and joy.

You'll also be subscribed to my newsletter and receive free giveaways, insights into my writing life, new release advance alerts and inspirational tips to help you live and work with passion, joy, and prosperity. Opt out at anytime.

COPYRIGHT

nature to help you in your quest for emotional, physical, and spiritual well-being.

Any use of information in this book is at the reader's discretion and risk. Neither the author nor the publisher can be held responsible for any loss, claim or damage arising out of the use, or misuse, of the suggestions made, the failure to take medical advice or for any material on third party websites.

ISBN PRINT: 978-0-9941484-7-6
ISBN EBOOK: 978-0-9941484-6-9
ISBN HARDCOVER: 978-0-9951289-0-3

Second Edition

www.ingramcontent.com/pod-product-compliance
Lightning Source LLC
Chambersburg PA
CBHW031938090426
42811CB00002B/232